Cybersecurity Exposed:

The Cyber House Rules

What is causing the frequency and magnitude of digital disruption to increase?

Is there a set of principles organizations can apply to prevent megabreaches?

Cybersecurity Exposed:

The Cyber House Rules

Raef Meeuwisse

Cyber Simplicity Ltd

2017

Raef Meeuwisse, Cyber Simplicity Ltd, Hythe, KENT, UK CT21 5HE.

Email:	orders@cybersimplicity.com
Twitter:	@RaefMeeuwisse
First Printing:	2016
ISBN	978-1-911452-09-6
First published by:	Cyber Simplicity Ltd
Edition Date:	28th November 2016
Publication Date:	2nd January 2017

www.cybersimplicity.com

www.cybersecurityexposed.com

www.thecyberhouserules.com

Ordering Information:

Special discounts are available on quantity purchases by corporations, associations, educators, and others. For details, contact the publisher at the above listed address. Trade bookstores and wholesalers: Please contact Cyber Simplicity Ltd.

Tel/Fax: +44(0)1227 540 540 or email orders@cybersimplicity.com.

Information is the primary security perimeter

Trusted public Internet-connected networks are history;

Great security is possible.

If you keep shooting the messengers,

they stop bringing you the information.

Also Available

Also available from this author in paperback & digital formats:

Cybersecurity for Beginners

This book provides an easy insight into the full discipline of cybersecurity, even if you have a non-technical background.

The Cybersecurity to English Dictionary

A useful companion for anyone who wants to keep up with cybersecurity terms or confound others with their understanding. Finally, cybersecurity does not need to sound like a different language.

The Encrypted Pocketbook of Passwords

Writing down your passwords is usually fraught with risks. The Encrypted Pocketbook of Passwords helps you to store your passwords more securely in a format that you can read but that others will find hard to break.

Cybersecurity: Home and Small Business

Guidance on the basic security practices we can apply at home or in small businesses to help decrease the risk of being successfully attacked.

Visit www.cybersimplicity.com for a full list of our latest titles

Looking for great corporate promotional gifts?

Check out our offers at **www.cybersimplicity.com**

Contents

Chapter Summary

1: The Cyber House Rules – introduces the issues and the set of rules that can be applied to overcome them.

2: The Cyber Pandemic – reviews the primary factors driving the increase in successful cyber attacks that are covered in more depth throughout this book.

3: Cybersecurity Basics – affirms the basic principles required when looking to achieve effective cybersecurity.

4: Security Psychology and the Medusa Effect – looks at the underlying psychological factors affecting executive boards and security managers that can keep substantial security gaps open.

5: Yesterday's Security Tomorrow – how the speed of change can create a cycle of opportunity for cyber criminals and other threat actors.

6: Security by Design – how introducing security from the outset can create efficient and effective security functions that operate at a fraction of the cost of reactive approaches.

7: Cybersecurity and Cybercrime Evolution – what is set to change and how quickly will it happen?

8: Blocking the Blockchain – what additional steps can be taken to help further reduce the incentives and motivation for cyber attacks? Will new regulations help?

9: Do You Have a Megabreach Brewing? – easy indicators for executives and business professionals that show an organization has clear vulnerability to major attacks.

10: Utopian Cybersecurity – Brings together the key principles from the book and reviews what an effective cybersecurity function looks like.

The Cybersecurity to English Dictionary (abridged) – defines key terms used in this book.

Introduction

Mind the gap... between the actual level of **cybersecurity** and the amount required to protect you.

Ever wondered what exactly is going so badly wrong in society that the fastest booming industry in the world is **cybercrime?**

Psychology meets technology as this book explores how the rapid progression of technology is luring us all forward at a pace that outstrips the human comfort zone.

This book exposes the reasons that many organizations decide it is cheaper, easier and less painful in the short term to leave their security broken, even when it can be fixed.

We take a look at **the cyber house rules,** a set of principles that lead to what makes cybersecurity effective or, if not addressed, leaves large gaps that cyber criminals, rogue insiders and other hostile parties can take advantage of.

Having written the security and privacy control frameworks for several multi-billion dollar companies and having reviewed security at more than fifty other organizations, I formulated a clear understanding about what is going wrong.

Added to that, the rise of **cryptocurrencies** such as **Bitcoin** means that many attackers can now directly monetize each attack using these currencies as leverage. Attackers no longer have to quietly try to re-sell their information to other criminals on the dark web. These attackers can now extort money directly from their victims, behind a shield of anonymity, with little fear of being traced.

... and even if you can trace your attackers, the likelihood is that they will be operating from a territory or country whose justice system is beyond the reach of most law enforcement agencies, so prosecuting them will be difficult to impossible.

So how do I know all of this?

The one good thing that was passed down from my dad to me was a few of his genes that specifically gave me his ability to understand and solve very complex problems very simply.

I can have dozens of seemingly disconnected pieces of information arrive at different times, but can instinctively 'see' exactly where and how they interconnect. And I do mean 'see'; if something interesting comes across my desk, it will literally 'glow' in the right places to let me know which data point (or data points) contain the clues for solving the problem.

Although there may be thousands of these data points, I have the ability to understand how they intersect and influence each other.

But I also have a major deficit. Although I can remember thousands of data points in my medium and long-term memory, I have incredibly poor short-term memory. If someone shows an individual a tray containing 9 items, removes 2 items, and asks him or her what is missing, most people can name at least one of the missing items, and some can name both. That's because a typical human has the ability to store between 5 and 9 pieces of information in short-term memory. Most cognition experts describe this as the ability of the average human to store seven, plus or minus two, pieces of information.

On a good day, I can remember 4. On a bad day it is 3.

As a consequence, I am a prolific note taker. It is the only way for me to ensure I will store all the information.

My short-term memory problem also makes me very prone to interrupt conversations. I can literally feel information falling out of my mind, so if I have a pressing question and no pad at hand on which to store it, out it comes. To me, this literally seems like my brain's request for other brains to help preserve the question.

If I take notes and review them, I can commit everything I need to remember to memory. And if I do that, those pieces of information tend to stay there... for a very, very long time – not just days, but years.

In a very real way, my brain is a bit of a manufacturing mistake. Its supernormal ability to retain long-term information, see the issues and solve multidimensional problems comes at the expense of requiring a pen and paper constantly at hand as a buffer for my frankly awful short-term recall.

However, being able to understand complex problems is not a valuable skill.

Even having the ability to provide simple and effective solutions is worth very little.

In a world run by humans, you cannot simply present a solution, even if it is fully correct – and then expect that to be enough for the solution to be adopted.

Understanding and navigating the rules and biases of the influential people we operate with – this skill is where the money is.

This means that to solve security issues, we must be equipped to understand not only the processes required to achieve our goals, but must also understand the organizational biases and obstacles that prevent those measures from being adopted.

Please note that cybersecurity terms that appear in ***bold italics*** when they are first used also have definitions that be found at the back of this book.

A larger and more comprehensive ***Cybersecurity to English Dictionary*** is also available as a separate publication.

cybersecurity – *the protection of **digital devices** and their communication channels to keep them stable, dependable and reasonably safe from danger or threat. Usually the required protection level must be sufficient to prevent or address unauthorized access or intervention before it can lead to substantial personal, professional, organizational, financial and/or political harm.*

digital device – *any electronic appliance that can create, modify, archive, retrieve or transmit information in an electronic format. Desktop computers, laptops, tablets, smartphones and Internet-connected home devices are all examples of **digital devices**.*

Cyber Attack Basics:

Hostile parties (***threat actors***)

seek

vulnerabilities (security gaps)

to

exploit (take advantage of)

for

financial or political gain.

1: The Cyber House Rules

The ability to adopt and use new technology quickly and safely is key to the long-term survival of any organization, commercial or otherwise.

With the rapid pace of technological change, ensuring the right controls are in place before anything new is scaled up for use is essential.

> Without exception, **every major cyber breach, when examined for its root cause, can always be attributed to the fact that at least 3 safeguards critical to security were either not in place or were not fit for purpose.**

What we look at in this book is how to understand whether your organization has those types of deficits and how to sensitively address them if needed.

We also take a very earnest look at what factors, especially human factors, often lead to a resistance to improve security. After all, so far, nobody has been fired for sitting on top of a risk that did not materialize during their tenure. Conversely, there are plenty of well-intentioned professionals who have been laid off or marginalized for shining a light, or for tackling major risks.

When Yahoo revealed it had over 500 million customer account details stolen, people looked to blame those who were in control at the point of disclosure. They did not seek accountability from those who were responsible at the time the breach took place. In fact, some of that management staff had already moved on to pastures new.

Organizations that bury security risk do get caught out in the long term. (Look at how the immediate value of Yahoo was affected after their breach was disclosed in 2016). However, the nature of cyber attacks encourages organizations with devastating security gaps to sit on them and to pass them forward in time.

This creates a massive problem for many organizations. Unless your security has been maintained at a robust level for a very long time, a sudden and successful move to improve security usually causes a greater short-term risk impact than leaving it buried does.

You may not think your organization has substantial security deficits. However, if your organization is of any reasonable size, you may well think it does by the end of this first chapter.

In 2016, the average length of time for a Chief Information Security Officer (CISO) to hold a position was just 17 months (source: www.cio.com). Considering that the CISO role is designed to be accountable for information leakage prevention, it should be clear that there are some big problems to tackle on this front.

The rapid and frequent changes of CISO can indicate one of 2 problems (or both):

1) The CISO was not deemed to be sufficiently competent for the role (indicating there were gaps in that organization's security).
2) The CISO was very security competent but could not gain sufficient support, confidence or maybe even access to the executive board to address the gaps.

Either of these situations is not good.

After meeting and knowing over a hundred different CISOs and even performing the role myself, I know that reason 2) occurs so often that it influences CISOs' behavior.

Specifically, executive boards often encourage CISOs to present a much rosier picture than actually exists. After all, if you make your management aware of the real situation, unless you possess incredible communication and boardroom political skills in addition to being a security expert, they will probably start looking to replace you.

Communication and boardroom politics are key skill requirements for any CISO who needs to sensitively transform and harden an organization's security.

A lot of companies think they are safe because they choose to purchase cyber insurance. I am keen to debunk that myth, since...

Insurers do not typically insure houses that are already burning.

Insurance companies have actually nailed the basics of security better than most organizations have. The typical cyber insurance policy amounts to this:

- You will be insured for any structured or unstructured information that is on an asset list...
- as long as each asset on that list has had an assessment, on a regular basis, to ensure it has the security in place that is appropriate to the value of the information it holds...
- and also provided that any major or critical gaps in the security have been adequately addressed.

Now remember, every megabreach, upon analysis, can always be attributed to 3 or more major gaps. Your cyber insurance is unlikely to do very much in that circumstance.

This is a good time to introduce some details about how these gaps occur.

Over the past 10 years, I have reviewed the security at over fifty different organizations. They have ranged from top 3 cloud service providers and other Fortune 500 companies, to Silicon Valley start-ups, to medium-sized Russian technology providers, right down to developers working from their basements.

During all those reviews, I saw a lot of really obvious, yet unstated patterns that could be useful as rules to guide security.

This is the set of rules I have developed to explain the challenges of cybersecurity and how to navigate resolving them:

The Cyber House Rules:

- Your information of value, and where you allow it to travel, defines where you need your security.

- If you are riddled with intruders, don't expect to just push them out, or they will attempt to destroy you.

- It is the gaps that get targeted, not the working defenses. Don't allow the security you do have to reassure you; find out what you don't have.

- Security is thousands of times cheaper when embedded by design from the earliest stage. Security is not a paint that can be applied at the end. Applying security later on is more expensive than starting over is.

- Any sensible cyber insurance will not cover the damage from gaps that you should have known about and fixed. Every major cyber breach, when examined for its root cause, can always be attributed to the fact that at least 3 safeguards critical to security were either not in place or were not fit for purpose.

- The security function exists to provide processes, technologies and advice that enable the business to operate within its preferred risk tolerance level. Security personnel should not make direct business decisions.

- Any organization that pays a ransom is supporting cybercrime. Any security professional who supports payment of a ransom is neither professional nor any good at security.

- Security measures must deliver tangible benefits and value that exceed both their direct and indirect costs, or they will not be implemented.

- Do not expect organizations to stop doing something just because it is illegal. They only stop when the near-term fines and consequences outweigh the remediation costs.

- Executive dynamics result in security function heads being incentivized by boards to bury risks more often than they are encouraged to resolve them. An effective CISO has to change that dynamic through soft skills (planning, communication and political maneuvering).

- If you have security risk information that is going to be way outside a group's comfort zone, you have to present it in stages, with solutions that form a comfortable trail. Only if you allow your audience's comfort zone to gradually change to the point that they can cope with the information will they be able to accept it. If you do not, then your audience will deny the situation exists, even if the facts prove otherwise.

- Executives invest in what they prefer, not what they need. Your job is to convince them to prefer what they need.

- One in 10 people click on phishing links. One in 3000 people click on every single link and open every document they receive. Do not expect those numbers to change; instead, fix the safeguards.

- Network security is now an oxymoron. Networks are no longer **the** security layer; they are only **a** partially effective security detection layer that covers only a fraction of the digital territory that any organization owns.

- The extent to which your last lines of cyber defense get triggered and used (for example, recovery management and information loss prevention alerts) is an effective measure of how many gaps you have in your primary security defenses.

- A skilled attacker knows your security weaknesses better than anyone in your company does.

- Criminals share information better and faster than legitimate organizations do.

- Do not employ active criminals within a security department. Using self-confessed, unreformed cyber criminals (grey hats) to operate security introduces an extreme insider threat.

- Anyone using **only** a published framework to manage security is using something that is already 2 or more years behind what is required.

- Guidance on security is rarely challenged. If you pay someone to give you security guidance, he or she will give you an answer with conviction, but it may not be correct or up to date. Verify that security guidance is up to date and valid before relying upon it.

- Your largest vulnerabilities often result from failing to put essential security processes in place. Your next-largest vulnerabilities result from failing to address the critical and major gaps that the processes identify.

- Fix the causes of security gaps before fixing the symptoms. There is no point in bailing water out of a boat riddled with holes. Fix key security processes and other root causes first, and then you can address the symptoms permanently without fear of them continually returning.

- Audit your security function each year through an independent party that has nothing to gain or sell through the outcome.

- Security is not everyone's responsibility, especially if they don't have the necessary skills or motivation. Skill them up and motivate them and many of them will help – but don't expect them to do your job.

- Always remember: employees do what optimizes their personal objectives and that can be (1) in conflict with the organization's objectives and (2) manipulated unless the right rules and consequences are in place. For example – people managing critical infrastructure systems are making decisions that can lead to loss of life with almost no fear of personal reprisals for getting it wrong.

- Your company does not know who really works for it or handles its information, when you consider suppliers, suppliers to your suppliers, cloud providers and other non-employees with the potential for privileged access.

- Trust-based systems make easy targets for cyber criminals. Proactive security control-based systems deliver the most effective defense.

- If there is not just one person with full accountability for something, there is nobody who is accountable for it. Shared accountability is no accountability.

- Encryption is a lock that degenerates over time. If you can sit and wait for long enough, you can undo any form of encryption.

- If you get the security team to score their own performance, don't expect full transparency and an honest result.

- Do not ask the turkeys to vote for Christmas. Leaving security decisions for creation and approval through the people it will negatively impact will not generate the required outcomes. People with the wrong skills and domain knowledge will not vote to replace themselves.

- Cryptocurrency enables most cybercrime. If (or when) the blockchain is defeated, the cybercrime industry will suffer a massive deflation.

- If you shoot the messengers, for some reason, they stop bringing you information.

Consider this real-world example of how security gaps can be created and perceived. This is based on a real security audit:

At a payroll services company, somewhere in Asia:

During a security audit for a new service managing very sensitive personal information, I was taken to see a door.

It was an amazing door. It was thick steel, it had multi-point bolts, there were 4 high definition CCTV cameras on each side, trained to capture images front, behind and each side of any person who used the door. Then there was a beautiful blue LED glow on the small console that could open this door. The door could only be opened using a combination of the palm print of an authorized employee, together with a unique personal identification number (PIN) known only to each authorized individual.

'Two factor authentication,' explained the company representative with a huge smile. It requires something you are (in this case the palm of your hand) and something you know (your secret PIN) to operate.

Each operation or attempted operation of the door was logged. The door was networked to a central security operations center and would automatically raise an alert for any unexpected, unauthorized or suspicious use.

On the floor itself, the payroll details for tens of thousands of people were processed each day. It really was a cutting-edge, high security door, for a high security location.

Along the same wall, there was another, identical door.

'These doors cost our client a fortune,' the company security representative announced proudly.

This was the kind of door executives display in demonstrations to help reassure stockholders about how seriously they treat security.

It was the most beautiful door I had ever seen. Carbon black, forged out of ultra-resilient materials, covered in tamper detection film, it felt like it could keep back any incursion. This was a door that easily cost a six figure sum… and there were two of them.

However, what I noticed was that nobody seemed to be using these doors. Sure, they had taken ME through one of them – but what was everyone else using?

I started to wander along the wall. The staff escorting me looked nervous. I turned around the corner and there was another door. This one was wide open. It had no fancy lock, just a push bar to open it. It was made of wood. There was no CCTV over it. People were using it as the main way in and out to the elevator, stairs and restrooms. 'Erm – why do you have this door? Doesn't it kind of make the other doors useless?' I asked.

The security representative looked at his shoes. 'There is a local fire regulation that the security doors cannot comply with. Every floor has to have doors that can be operated by a simple exit push bar in case of emergency,' he admitted.

It turned out that a customer who demanded that the high security doors had to be installed had been unwilling to hear about the local fire regulation. 'They were very explicit about the specification of the doors they wanted fitted,' the security representative explained. So the payroll services company had fitted the doors just as requested and sent them the bill.

Of course, they left the regulation fire doors in place too.

Clearly, those high security doors were useless. You would need to be an incredible idiot to target a couple of reinforced steel, multi-factor authentication, CCTV covered doors, when there was an open and unmonitored wooden door just around the corner.

The physical security deficiency here is exactly like the cybersecurity deficiencies that exist in most organizations.

Most organizations spend an absolute fortune on delivering some very robust security in one direction, only to leave a large number of gaping security holes elsewhere that negate those expensive efforts.

A fortune is spent in the areas at which the security people remember to look.

On the other hand, the attackers are not looking at what you do have. They are looking for what the security folks forgot to look at...

Now you may still (at this point) be feeling that there is a chance your security is robust. Maybe you don't have the equivalent of the security fire door gap that I found at the payroll services supplier. So here is the kicker:

When a gap is found in software or hardware, it opens up a hole (vulnerability) that can be taken advantage of by various cyber criminals and other hostile parties.

At the point when the manufacturer knows about the hole, it is possible that the hostiles do not. However, when the manufacturer releases the fix for the hole to their clients, all of the hostiles also get to know about it. Twenty-four hours from the point when a patch (the fix from the manufacturer) is released, the hostiles are able to 'buy' the exploit that can get into those systems that have not had the manufacturer's fix (the patch) applied.

So that means that even if you only allow a 48 hour window between patches being released and applied, your systems will be open to attack for 24 hours.

Now ask yourself this – what is the time permitted at your organization between the release of patches from the manufacturer and the deployment of those patches?

For most organizations, it is still measured in weeks, and some leave their devices unpatched for months or years.

2: The Cyber Pandemic

Weak Security

I sat down opposite a friend of mine and asked him this: 'Do you still trust banks? I mean with your money?'

I asked this question because, like other businesses, banks are being increasingly targeted by cyber criminals. You might have noticed that the state of cybersecurity is not improving. The breaches, attacks and impacts are getting larger. Several recent events involved:

- Billions of account passwords stolen directly from major brands.
- About $1 billion stolen from a group of banks via their ATMs.
- Major Internet outages for leading online sites and services...

It does not seem to matter how large and powerful the target is, nothing seems invincible to the power of a cyber attack.

It may seem to be very difficult to be an effective protector who must offer a robust and unbroken line of defense against everything.

Conversely, it can appear to be pretty easy to be a hacker or other attacker. You only need to find one weakness in your opponent's digital landscape to get in.

In October 2016 *The Guardian*, a British newspaper, published an article stating that a number of blue-chip banks were accumulating **Bitcoin**s (a **cryptocurrency**) in case they were needed to pay ransoms. Bitcoins are the leading form of payment for cybercrime. They allow ransoms to be paid without disclosing the recipient's information.

These banks had assessed their security, weighed the cost of ransom payments against the cost of resolving the intrusions themselves, and made the mother of all bad decisions: **that it would be cheaper to pay up**.

In 2013, a report by the FBI estimated that some 90% of all Bitcoin transactions were directly related to crime. Any organization that pays a ransom is effectively supporting cybercrime.

I would certainly advise anyone to actively move their business away from any organization that supports cybercrime.

However, the fact that some banks are willing to concede defeat and pay money is a clear example of how bad the cyber situation is.

Many banks' security is so bad, they paper over the security gaps by providing payments to cyber criminals to allow the banks to keep operating.

You would think that if you were so bad at your job that the only way forward was to admit defeat and allow attacks to continue, you might look for a new career. But this is the real world – and in the real world, if you are paid to do something and there are little to no personal consequences for doing it badly, people just keep going in the same direction.

Worse still, there are huge personal consequences for people who admit defeat or who step up and challenge bad security ideas.

In effect, most security managers are paid more to continue in the same direction that is allowing cybercrime to boom than they would be paid if they attempted to address and correct the issues.

Tell an executive board the truth about their security position and most security function heads will be out of a well-paid job.

However, if you can make an executive board feel comfortable with remaining at high risk, you will have a job for a much longer time… well, at least until the really big risk hits.

I meet people who work in bank security. You may or may not be surprised to know that quite a few of them refuse to hold any significant amount of their own funds in the banks for which they provide security services. They don't trust the security they see.

There are many excellent security professionals out there. However, most of them are encouraged to keep relatively quiet about the known security issues and to find the cheapest temporary workarounds.

One CISO gave the analogy that trying to operate within his security budget was like trying to spread the contents of a peanut butter jar over the face of the planet.

As I explained this to my friend, who is, incidentally, also a police officer, he shifted uncomfortably in his chair.

'Do you really think it is that bad?' he asked.

As most security professionals know, yes, it really is that bad. If you are a security professional reading this book, you probably have a good grasp of how things are in your own organization. How many systems are left without the latest patches in place for weeks, months or even years? You probably know how much really sensitive information that should be adequately encrypted is not. How many applications with massive security gaps are still being relied upon because the cost to check, repair or replace them has not yet been approved?

These problems are endemic. There is almost no environment without them.

Technology is outpacing the traditional investment models. Something bought 3 years ago is now well out of date – but organizations are not geared up to handle this rate of change.

Of course, it is actually possible to run security well. It is also relatively inexpensive, if robust and sensible security is added from the outset.

> • *Security is thousands of times cheaper when embedded by design from the earliest stage. Security is not a paint that can be applied at the end. Applying security later on is more expensive than starting over is.*

As an example, if you look at the ***Distributed Denial of Service*** (DDoS) attacks that started to take place in late 2016, they leveraged the incredibly poor security that had been hard-coded into a number of low-cost devices that connect to the Internet. CCTV cameras, recorders and other 'Internet of Things' devices had been released and sold with mistakes as simple as shipping them out with standard, default and often unchangeable usernames and passwords.

It was easy for anyone to then access them, insert their own malicious software and then hijack at least part of their bandwidth as part of an army (a ***botnet***). This army could then point an overwhelming amount of data transactions at any point on the Internet. A super canon of trashy requests that then prevented the legitimate services from running.

Manufacturers of these devices had 2 choices. Run away and disown the problem, or pay for a very expensive recall and repair.

It is easy to see that if someone had been looking at the basics of security during the initial design stage, one of the most basic controls they would have applied would have been not to use default usernames and passwords – and definitely not to hard code them (make them unchangeable). That simple measure would have cost a few thousand dollars at most at the outset. The consequences and impact of not doing it run to at least tens of millions of dollars.

What leaves organizations open to running security badly is that it initially appears to be cheaper and easier to do it that way. After all, most of the risk is not with the organization, it transfers to the customers and others.

When Talk Talk, a UK communications provider, ran what can only be described as truly eye wateringly poor security that allowed over a hundred thousand customers' details (including bank account numbers and dates of birth) to be stolen in October 2015 – they were given a fine that amounted to the equivalent of $509,298 – a fraction of what they should have been spending on the security they did not have in place.

Fortunately, some change is coming. The European Union is passing a new General Data Protection Regulation (the GDPR) into law in May 2018. Anybody expecting to deal with EU citizens' data after that time will be facing a fine of up to 4% of their global revenue (revenue, not profit) if they turn out to be mismanaging personal information.

> • *Do not expect organizations to stop doing something just because it is illegal. They only stop when the near-term fines and consequences outweigh the remediation costs.*

This substantial increase in potential penalties, and other similar regulations, are now leading many organizations to take security more seriously.

However, the upgrades in the security budget will be too late for quite a few major organizations. There will undoubtedly be some very dramatic examples of companies being brought down due to their security.

The current situation in almost all organizations is that the security teams and security investments are hopelessly mired in what amounts to more of a marketing exercise than a truly effective cybersecurity program. They don't actually want the expense of fixing the security; they just want to portray the image of working in the right direction.

Easy-to-deploy technologies like data loss prevention, which should act as a last line of defense (when all else fails), are heralded as the magic bullets that they are not. At the same time, the organizations that use these inappropriate stopgap measures are running on ecosystems of technologies that are rich with gaps that can easily be taken advantage of by savvy cyber criminals and other hostile parties.

If that is not bad enough – even if you find a rare organization that has a solid and well-invested security position, the criminals still only need to find their way into the account of someone with valid, authorized access to achieve an initial foothold.

One of the most frequently seen security gaps is that the organization is led to believe that holding a single, accurate inventory of its information assets is a nearly impossible task. It is actually pretty easy. It only requires a very simple process, executive mandate and register.

Yet, because there is some truth to the fact that you cannot make everything impenetrable, that fact is used to disguise the deficits that could have been easy to resolve.

Organizations that genuinely think BYOD (Bring Your Own Device) is a good money-saving policy provide an easy example of companies that don't really understand security or take it seriously. It is impossible to lock down security on the tens of thousands of different devices that can be used – so essentially any information allowed into an open BYOD framework is open to theft. And if you limit devices to a small number of specific devices owned by the company – that is great – but is not really bringing your own device, right?

Ironically, even the UK government's advice on BYOD is pretty much to not do it. It advises that you can do BYOD, but that you should be careful about what information you allow onto them – and that you should consider limiting information you really care about to only being allowed on devices your organization selects, controls and owns.

Given the security deficiencies that exist in most organizations, you may be told that security is hard to achieve. That is not true. The truth is that security only becomes expensive and resource-heavy when it is applied like paint later on. If you apply strong security by design from the very beginning, security can bring returns that outweigh its costs.

Think about it – what happens to brands and companies that repeatedly demonstrate they have security that gets bypassed in major ways on more than one occasion? They lose customers and market value.

In the next chapter, you will see just how easy security can be – if basic security processes are applied consistently.

Indifference

How much does the average person care about cybersecurity?

One of the most frequently used but widely ignored slogans is 'Security is everybody's responsibility.'

It just isn't. Not if you are just an average person going about his or her business. If you are the average person, you probably know close to nothing about cybersecurity. You just want to get on with what you need to do.

Besides, if a security team cannot tell the difference between a good link or file attachment and one that leads to a malware infection – what makes that the problem of the user?

Is it impossible for the security team to implement safeguards between the dangerous content in some incoming emails and the legitimate information assets that need to be protected? No, it is not impossible. You can run next generation endpoint security, run virtual browsers, use safe link filtering software and more...

The average person is very happy to do really basic things to help an organization's security position. He or she is not, however, a security expert. Such individuals are largely unable to differentiate between good and bad content, especially when the security technologies in place do nothing to help them make this distinction or to prevent a poor decision from wrecking a section of a computer network.

> - *Security is not everyone's responsibility, especially if they don't have the necessary skills or motivation. Skill them up and motivate them and many of them will help – but don't expect them to do your job.*

One way in which security professionals can educate and engage other employees in helping to safeguard company security is by providing tips about how to secure personal devices. In fact, I can provide 4 simple steps right now that reduce the risk of a cyber attack on your personal device by over 90%:

- Keep your device and its software up to date with the latest updates (patches) from the manufacturers.
- Do not allow any account you routinely use to have the administrative rights to install new software. Keeping this permission isolated to a separate account will mean you have to at least use a separate password to confirm when you want new software installed.
- Make sure you have an up-to-date anti-malware solution installed.

- Back up your data to a separate location regularly.

Over 90% of **malware** (malicious software) cannot install unless the user has out-of-date software and is running with built-in permission to install new software. Anti-malware stops a significant amount of 'known' malware threats. Backing up data means that if you are caught out, you can recover without losing electronic information or paying a ransom.

Yet, despite the volume of cybercrime - the vast majority of people, even technical professionals, do not do these 4 things. Do you? Will you?

One reason few people take steps to secure their personal devices is that megabreaches have become so common that few people really pay attention to them. When a coordinated attack across a number of global banks resulted in the theft of a billion dollars, major news outlets barely publicized it when it was reported in February 2015. Even the targeted banks did not want to make much of a fuss; after all, they did not want their customers to lose confidence. The attackers made sure they hit each bank for less than $10 million so as not to make each loss unbearable, and in return, the banks decided that it was better to cover the losses than to highlight them. These thieves targeted ATM machines using malware known as Carbanak, turning these devices into remotely-controlled money dispensers for collection by their gangs.

You should ask yourself how the security of such a critical service could be allowed to be compromised. The answer is that it would not have been possible if the security had been adequately designed in the first place.

As this example demonstrates, cyber attacks barely make the news, even if they impact millions of people or result in financial losses in the tens of millions of dollars.

We all expect to have security embedded by design. When it is not, we all react with indifference and accept the list of excuses offered by the affected institutions.

Keep in mind that there is no megabreach in history (in which millions of account details or emails were stolen) that will turn out not to have resulted from

3 or more standard security controls failing to be effective or failing to be present.

> • *Any sensible cyber insurance will not cover the damage from gaps that you should have known about and fixed. Every major cyber breach, when examined for its root cause, can always be attributed to the fact that at least 3 safeguards critical to security were either not in place or were not fit for purpose.*

One of the main things we can all do is to demand security by design and to abandon platforms and services in which it does not happen. If an organization is transferring their security gaps to individuals, vote with your feet and leave them.

If you are still not convinced that indifference is a large part of the problem – consider this anecdote from a security conference:

A security team tried an experiment. They placed 12 USB storage keys in a cupboard that held stationery, each one marked with the words 'INFECTED – do not use.'

The USB keys were not infected. They did have a small program on them that plugging in the device triggered. The program would simply take the name of the user who was logged in to the device and send it to the security team.

Twenty-four hours after being placed in the cupboard, six of the devices had been plugged in and had reported back to the security team.

Remember, even if over 99% of your user population does the right thing, that still means that in a large organization, some people will do the wrong thing.

> • One in 10 people click on phishing links. One in 3000 people click on every single link and open every document they receive. Do not expect those numbers to change; fix the safeguards instead.

Easy, Anonymous Money

The ease with which money can be made through cybercrime makes it a pretty compelling choice in certain areas of the world. People can transform their lives at the expense of faceless people and corporations in other parts of the world.

Imagine you have the choice between living on the breadline on a very low income on which you can hardly exist, or being relatively wealthy, at the expense of groups of people in far-off countries.

Added to that, consider how likely you might be to go down that route if you have been encouraged to think of those victims as privileged and able to afford these crimes.

I am in no way defending these crimes. However, the steep disparity in average living conditions found between different nations, coupled with the financial lure of these activities, means that we should not expect to be able to police our way out of the situation.

The majority of cybercrime *is* committed from offshore and mostly from poorer countries. Only amateurs would look to hack in the same geographic territory where they might face consequences. Skilled hackers can earn more money in developed countries working on security than they can trying to earn from crime.

The fact is that even if the police could identify who did what to whom – they could do close to nothing about crimes that were committed from other countries and territories. The victim might be local – but the chances are very high that the criminal behind the crime is not.

Added to this problem, if you live in a country where cybercrime is an acceptable way of life, it takes hardly any time or training to step on the bandwagon to start earning from it.

The overall result is that cybercrime is not only the fastest growth industry in the world, it is also worth hundreds of billions of any currency you care to name.

The World Economic Forum estimated that the cybercrime industry earned $445 billion in 2016. That means it earned more money than the entire economies of any single country ranked 26th or lower in the world.

And driving this lucrative crime industry is cryptocurrency.

A cryptocurrency is essentially like any other form of money. It has a value. But instead of being transacted between identified individuals and organizations, the owner of any particular account simply owns a specific private key. Rather than being physical, the key is also electronic. If the owner loses the key, he or she can never recover access to the account.

Cyptocurrencies have not only driven the huge rise in cybercrime, but have also led to tremendous increases in criminals extorting money directly from their victims, mostly through the use of ransomware.

Before cryptocurrencies caught on, cybercrime was easy to achieve but much more difficult to turn into profitable business ventures. Criminals could get in relatively easily, but had to rely on re-selling stolen information to other criminals to turn a profit. The combination of ransomware and cryptocurrency substantially changed and accelerated the money model.

Ransomware operates by literally locking a victim away from his or her own information or access to his or her own devices or accounts unless he or she pays the criminal to get it restored.

If you pay a ransom, not only does the criminal earn immediate money, but he or she can also sell your details so other criminals know that you are someone who pays up. You essentially get added to a sucker list. That means if you fall for this attack and pay up once, the likelihood is that it will happen again and again.

As you read earlier in this chapter, it is not actually that difficult to prevent becoming a victim of this type of attack. Relatively simple security steps can almost eliminate the risk. Sadly, these are not steps that are automatically built into most of the Internet-accessible devices and services we currently buy and use.

Weak security and general apathy were already providing a lot of opportunities for criminals. However, the major change has been fueled by criminals' ability to receive money internationally and anonymously through cryptocurrency.

A lot of people are heralding the arrival of something called '***blockchain***' as a huge step forward in our ability to achieve better security. The reality is that blockchain, a technology that enables cryptocurrency to operate, is largely responsible for the tremendous rise in cybercrime.

Here is a simplified explanation of how blockchain works:

- Each account holder has 2 keys. A public key, that can be openly known and used to send money to an account, and a private key that allows anyone with it to view the balance or make payments from the account.
- Whenever money is transferred, the legitimate transaction is stored as an audit trail item in the digital blockchain ledger. That audit trail item includes the sender's public key information, the recipient's public key information, the amount transferred and a special security feature that makes use of something called a ***hash*** value.
- The hash value is a set of characters that is generated using a special algorithm. If you run the algorithm over any set of electronic information, it will only return the same value if all of the characters are identical. If even a single character is changed, the hash value will be completely different. The unique hash value is not based only on the single audit trail item – but also on the full content of the audit trail item directly before it.
- Because the audit trail item directly before it also contains a hash value, each audit trail item acts like an impenetrable link in a chain.
- The blockchain ledger further secures the audit trail against unauthorized modification by running in a confederated (distributed) model. There are hundreds of thousands of versions of the ledger. A new transaction can start on any one of these versions and only becomes fully validated once more than 50% of the ledgers have accepted the entry.

- Each ledger, run by a bitcoin 'miner,' can verify each transaction by checking the hash value to verify whether the entry is valid and acceptable.
- Due to the large number of audit trail copies, the potential to adjust the audit trail theoretically requires too much access, knowledge and computing power to be possible.
- Therefore each 'block' (audit trail item) is chained to the one before it in an unbreakable, distributed chain.

Entries are not made using peoples' names; they only use the equivalent of a public numbered account (a public cryptography key). Only the secret private key can be used to authorize payments out of an account. One or more private keys can be held inside the digital equivalent of a wallet.

If someone steals a legitimate private key (and they know which public key it works with) they effectively have full access to that Bitcoin account.

Blockchain enables transactions to be made directly between 2 parties without an accountable middleman being required.

Commercial and government organizations are looking at how they can leverage this technique to improve security. Almost everyone believes it will not be defeated. I do not agree. I can already think of ways to defeat Blockchain, given enough computing power and permission!

If there are two things I have learned about impenetrable audit trails, it is this – (i) they are usually not impenetrable and (ii) you only need to insert rubbish as legitimate transactions for the entire system to fail.

- *Cryptocurrency enables most cybercrime. If (or when) blockchain gets defeated, the cybercrime industry will suffer a massive deflation.*

Accountable middle parties help to ensure that rogue transactions, like the ones that support cybercrime, cannot take place.

This decentralized and unregulated method of payment is the primary cause of the boom in cybercrime. Criminals can now take money straight from their victims more easily than they could through other means.

Anti-Social Engineering

Okay, so this is usually described as '***social engineering***' but the reality is that these are ploys that use social manipulation to sucker people into revealing private information or providing hostile parties with access to personal accounts or organizations' computer networks.

The tactics used range from very simple to very clever.

The easiest way around all security is to gain the trust of someone who has legitimate access. People with very senior and privileged access are even more attractive targets. These more attractive targets can range from CEOs right down to server administrators.

One way of targeting certain groups is by selecting them based on their location or office and then sending a fictitious voucher for 50% off a meal at a local restaurant. The PDF file with the fictional voucher can carry an unexpected passenger of malicious software. This is an example of a typical, very simple ***phishing*** technique.

More advanced techniques can reflect cyberattackers' knowledge about a target's psychology. Attackers spend time collecting information about the target and about his or her preferences, interests and needs.

For the highest value targets, the tactics can get really clever. Cyber criminals go to security conferences. They even specifically go to bars near certain places of work and recruit insiders, in ways that may or may not let the insider know that he or she is being recruited. These kinds of tactics are only worthwhile for the really high value targets.

What happens more frequently is that social engineering goes for the easy money. Perhaps you are lonely and they can provide the attention and company you crave?

It is not uncommon for people to be blackmailed for access or to be directly taken for large sums of cash by tricks that exploit their confidence in the cyber criminal.

According to 2016 statistics released by the UK Police Action Fraud unit, a staggering 68% of UK adults revealed that they had been targeted by cyber-crime at some point, with 39% of those choosing not to report the crime.

One way in which cyber criminals blackmail people is through an increasing number of online romance scams. Criminals find these scams to be an easy way of extracting large amounts of cash from each victim. One woman shared her story of being 'love bombed' out of more than $300,000 in the hope that it would act as a warning to others. These criminals study their victims' online information, seek to befriend them and then maximize the value they manipulate from their targets.

Sadly, once you fall for one ploy, that information tends to get shared and you will be targeted for more.

Social engineering can also take the form of a phone call from someone pretending to be from a legitimate organization, such as a bank, which already has part of your information and supposedly needs you to do something urgently, like confirming your account password to help investigators track down someone who tried to access your account.

Or criminals might send you a letter through the regular snail mail, requiring you to go to a particular web address to process something to prevent a fine or receive a payment.

However, the really clever social engineers looking at super high value targets look deeply into the psychology of their subject and then construct something compelling for them. That merger you are about to commit to – suddenly some new information comes to light from a legitimate source. You open the file and...

As we improve technical security, forms of attack that rely on social engineering will increasingly focus on people with legitimate access to digital systems. They already happen a lot through techniques such as phishing emails and messages.

That self-driving car you bought. It might be locked to only respond to you through impenetrable security verification. That means a criminal needs to get you to instruct it to do what he or she wants.

If I were a criminal, I might not be able to *steal* $1,000 from you. It might be easier to convince you to just give it to me.

The Speed of Change

You may have noticed that technology is changing civilization faster than at any other point in human history.

A few months ago, if I wanted to view a one hundred inch screen on my wall at home, I would have had to physically buy one. Now I can just buy a Microsoft Hololens and carry around the ability to view a screen that size anywhere I choose.

However, that physical screen might have lasted for well over a decade. My augmented reality device will be outdated within a year, and I probably will not be able to obtain security patches within a few years after that.

Technology is about to do the same thing to cars. Electric, self-driving cars will replace almost all traditional cars within the next ten years. The new cars will mostly be rented by the journey. Instead of cars that last for ten years or more and expect to run perhaps 10 to 20 thousand miles each year – the new cars will cover a few hundred thousand miles in just two or three years and then be scrapped or recycled.

Organizations are used to buying technology that will last them for a reasonable number of years before it is retired. Their financial models are built around this assumption. But models like this are rapidly being consigned to history.

Even a few years ago, the security of any organization was largely controllable by applying security primarily to the physical computer networks it owned. Now, any competitive organization has its information and dependency spread far outside any network it owns. It relies on Internet-based services, mobile devices, suppliers and customer devices over which it has very little direct control.

> • *Network security is now an oxymoron. Networks are no longer **the** security layer; they are only **a** partially effective security detection layer that covers only a fraction of the digital territory that any organization owns.*

It used to take tens of years for something new to get adopted by the mass market. Now anything new that is rapidly scalable and offers substantial benefits can go from concept to widespread usage in just a few years.

Take the smartphone as an example. In 2007, the Apple iPhone was initially treated skeptically; who wanted to carry the Internet around? Yet within 4 years, over half the market had moved to using it or something close to identical in functionality.

In practical terms, that means that the way we all work and live is changing at a speed that defies the traditional models on which we have been taught to rely.

In just ten year's time, we will not be carrying around large laptop computers, or sitting at desks with monitors, or even carrying smartphones with screens. We will be carrying around miniature devices with the power to offer access to virtual, mixed reality screens and interfaces which place sounds and images exactly where we want them.

Security will increasingly be embedded by design in these items. However, right now we all have a willingness to cling to what we know for as long as possible – and to extract all the residual value we can from what we have.

My four-year-old tablet device is effectively a pile of junk. Its manufacturer long since gave up on updating the operating system. Its processor is too slow to cope with new software. I can use it for basic web research, but I cannot trust or rely on it to manage any secure transactions. Not even the email on it would be safe. It is wide open to a huge array of cyber attacks.

Now imagine the situation in large organizations. They have critical systems that took them years to develop. They cannot replace them quickly or easily – but the likelihood is that those systems are reliant, in many places, on technology that is no longer supported and on security concepts that have long since been defeated.

A good example is that the level of password encryption considered robust six years ago can now be cracked simply by entering the encrypted value into a Google search. The unencrypted value will then be displayed in the search results, courtesy of something known as a *rainbow table*.

> • *Encryption is a lock that degenerates over time. If you can sit and wait for long enough, you can undo any form of encryption.*

To keep on top of security now requires people and organizations to live with technology lifecycles that are so fast, they are uncomfortable.

So what do we mean by the term technology lifecycle? New technologies are conceived, developed, released and retired. This cradle-to-grave process is a technology lifecycle, which requires different security considerations at each point along the journey.

You may have heard of something called 'the comfort zone'. This is the human propensity to keep operating within reasonable reach of what we know and can cope with. Most of us are content to operate within or close to our comfort zone. Conversely, as soon as someone is pushed too far outside their comfort zone – they just find a reason to retreat from the intrusion and get back into what they know.

Although technology and information security people always expected to have to adapt to new technologies, the lightning-fast speed at which technology is changing is now well outside of their own comfort zone. The natural reaction for most people is to resist change and to stay with what is known.

Until ten years ago, security was all about how you applied it to a network of private devices. Most in-house technology and security experts learned about internal networks. Yet most of the demands are now in all kinds of technologies and services that have little to do with internal networks.

Ten years back, cybercrime rates were low and so, comparatively, were connection speeds. It was possible that about 5% or less of your knowledge would need to be updated each year to keep pace with developments.

By 2016, any security professional needs to devote at least 20% of his or her time to continuous learning and skills development to sustain his or her value to the industry.

But this does not just affect security personnel. It starts at the very top of each organization. Boardroom executives must be persuaded to adopt greater agility in understanding and responding to the changes demanded by the need to quickly adjust to technology and its security requirements.

At a point where the incidence of cybercrime is doubling annually, the security strategy and investment has to reflect the increased threat levels.

Stick with outdated technology and you will be left behind and remain vulnerable to attacks. Adopt new technology without embedding the right safeguards and you are still vulnerable. The only safe route is to adopt new technologies with security embedded by design and then to invest sufficiently to keep that security sustained.

One day, something is an effective form of security. The next day, someone has found a way around it. For a brief period of time, the fix is unavailable. These are of course known as ***zero-day vulnerabilities***.

Between the time that the vulnerability is known and it is fixed, there is a period of opportunity for cyber criminals.

> • *Criminals share information better and faster than legitimate organizations do.*

The criminals quickly leverage these new gaps. Even if the gaps are discovered by the manufacturer, as soon as they are announced to the customer base, modules that take advantage of them are available to cyber criminals and other hostile parties within a matter of hours.

Manufacturers thus try to keep any information about gaps secret until they release the fix.

A great example of this happened as I was writing this book. Someone developed a USB stick that took advantage of the fact that the USB port is active, even when a screen lock is in place. If someone plugs the device into the side of a locked machine, the program runs, and 13 seconds later, ta da – one unlocked desktop or laptop device, ready to use.

The two main defenses against this are to install patches as soon as they are available (not days or weeks later) – and also to never rely on a single security measure.

In the scheme of all things security, zero-day threats are the one big thing that require a rapid reaction time, once the rest of a security system is up to snuff.

Unsurprisingly, leaving zero-day vulnerabilities open for weeks, months or years is still a common practice in too many companies.

Running software that is no longer supported has been a contributing factor to many megabreaches.

The Silver Lining

So if you have weak security that is full of gaps, indifference from users, motivated cyber criminals and rapid changes to technology that constantly open up new gaps, what hope is there?

Plenty.

The organizations that adopt robust security processes to embed security by design into a lifecycle that constantly identifies and (safely) adopts new technologies will win this battle.

This provides a real opportunity for many organizations to grow into the spaces being left by the other organizations that cannot cope with the changing threat landscape.

The factors outlined in this chapter help to describe the perfect storm creating the cyber pandemic. Executive boards that take the time to understand these factors can learn how to navigate the storm and incentivize their security functions to operate correctly.

Security people generally know what to do and how to do it. If they are motivated to identify and fix the problems, they will do so.

But most security functions are encouraged not to expose the true risks to their boards. If and when they do, they are punished.

> • *If you shoot the messengers, for some reason, they stop bringing you information.*

Bringing any organization to a much safer and lower level of cyber risk begins by having a culture that *actively* promotes identifying and addressing security issues.

3: Cybersecurity Basics

You may think all security professionals have a consistent view of the security basics. You are correct if you think all of them *should* share the same perspective. After all, effective cybersecurity is simply about understanding which appropriate security you need to have in place and then providing your organization with the right processes and resources to make it happen at the right time, followed by monitoring emerging risks and taking appropriate additional remediative actions.

However, if you put ten security experts in a room and ask them to describe the basics of the discipline, you might get ten unique and different answers. It all depends on each individual's experience and perspective.

Even if you give each of these ten people the same initial training, the way they perceive and manage problems will be shaped by the organizations for which they work. Each environment differs enormously in what is considered the acceptable way to manage practical security and security risk.

To illustrate this: One company might have staff members who would be devastated if someone casually pointed out that they had a minor typo in an otherwise perfect process document. Another company's employees would shrug as if to say 'so what' when someone found out they used shared administrative accounts over an Internet platform, through an offshore provider to manage sensitive information. Such employees might respond to criticism by stating, 'It would be impractical for us to work any other way.'

This was one of the first epiphany moments for me after carefully analyzing the security at more than fifty different organizations. I realized that there were huge perceptual differences about acceptable practices between organizations. No matter whether the security is run well or badly, the security staff will, with absolute conviction, assert that their company runs security correctly. The proof of this, the staff believes, lies in the fact that they are still employed. How could they be wrong?

For this reason, it is important to recap some of the very basic foundations of effective cybersecurity.

Cybersecurity Purpose

An effective cybersecurity department understands that it performs an enabling function. It does not make business decisions; in fact it is only present to provide the security processes, track the security metrics and help resolve the security issues that collectively allow each organization to operate within whatever risk tolerance levels it deems acceptable.

In other words, effective security allows an organization's employees to do their work without being unacceptably disrupted or damaged by the technologies they use.

In many ways, this role is similar to that of a finance department. Finance specialists do not make every purchase decision – but they are responsible for setting the rules, processes and limitations to ensure that all financial transactions, including budget requests, have the right checks, balances and approvals in place.

You would expect a finance department to have processes in place for all financial transactions and to always be aware of the organization's financial situation. Likewise, you would expect a security department to have processes in place to embed and sustain appropriate security measures throughout business activities and to always be aware of the security situation.

This means that the main function of any cybersecurity department is to allow the business to operate securely.

The employees responsible for making business decisions need robust processes and professional guidance to be able to carry out this part of their job, and it is the security department that provides these processes, security technologies, security metrics and advice that allows the business to operate within a comfortable level of security risk tolerance.

Security does not make decisions about what the business can and cannot do; it simply provides the processes that allow the risks to be understood and escalated further if appropriate.

There is another important element in this setup which ensures that the business management and security departments continue to serve the business in mutually beneficial ways. This element is an independent auditing company that evaluates the interactions between the business management and security departments at regular intervals.

What has been described above is a typical business model known as the 3 lines of defense model, in which:

1. The business management staff makes the decisions.
2. The security function provides processes and guidance.
3. A regular, independent auditing company checks that the security function is meeting the needs of the business – and that the business is adhering to the processes provided for it.

So, whenever the business needs something new, the security function has to assess whether the new item can be managed through existing security processes or requires the security team to establish new security processes.

Let's look at a specific example. Imagine that a group of people in an organization is looking to set up a new Facebook group. You would expect a process to be in place to help ensure that security is considered from the outset and that whatever security measures are implemented remain updated as long as the group exists.

Without security being embedded into that setup and management process, it would be easy for security gaps to appear because of the following conditions:

- The business decision-makers may not know there are security settings that can be configured – and may set them incorrectly. Should all the group members be able to see each other? Does joining require approval? Is a consent statement required? …
- The individuals who seek to join the new group may share certain qualities that subject the group to heightened security risks and even to privacy regulations, and this may in turn unintentionally subject the business which harbors the group members' electronic information to increased security risks. For example, the group members may all be

HIV positive or may all be in another vulnerable situation which requires heightened privacy protections.

- The lack of a sufficient budget allocation that provides the resources
to manage the group, including checking on content and issues that
arise, may also lead to security gaps.
- Not knowing how long the group will exist and not planning for its re-
tirement can endanger security.
- A failure to plan for the eventual placement of any data collected –
and not checking on the security of those locations... another path to
security gaps.

A process to verify security for social media platforms can be placed into a relatively simple, easy-to-use, and repeatable security plan that the business
groups themselves can access.

Each time someone with appropriate authority in the business wants to set up
a new social media group, they just need an easy and accessible way to register
their desire to set up a new information asset – and for that registration to trigger the right process to check that what they are doing is appropriate,
sufficiently planned and realized.

The role of the security function is only effective when it reflects an understanding of the importance of building scalable, easy-to-access processes for
the business that consistently trigger and sustain the inclusion of appropriate
security. Security is only responsible for security when the business follows the
rules and processes provided for it.

> - *The security function exists to provide processes, technologies and advice that enable
> the business to operate within their preferred risk tolerance level. Security personnel
> should not make direct business decisions.*

It is the responsibility of the audit function and the executive to chase down
any parts of the business that decide not to follow the rules.

The number one foundational process that allows effective security management is ensuring that every critical information asset and service is consistently
required to be registered in a single repository designated by management as

the only appropriate place for such information. After all, wherever any information for which your organization is responsible flows constitutes the locations where you need to provide appropriate security.

> • *Your information of value, and where you allow it to travel, defines where you need your security.*

Organizations with an accurately maintained information asset register in place are not concerned by regulations like the EU General Data Protection Regulation. They know what they need to look after and how to trigger appropriate follow-on processes to verify that effective safeguards are in place, even if the information for which they are responsible resides with a supplier or with some other external cloud or similar service.

Cyber Attack Basics

On the page that immediately precedes Chapter 1 (p.   ), I presented a very basic cyber attack model:

Hostile parties (***threat actors***)

seek

vulnerabilities (security gaps)

to

exploit (take advantage of)

for

financial or political gain.

There are many different types of hostiles out there:

- Cyber criminals
- Hacktivists
- Nation States
- Rogue insiders
- Amateurs

It is also important to note that some data loss can be accidental. There are plenty of cases in which people send information in bulk (information they arguably should not have been able to pull together) to unintended recipients and sometimes through unsecure channels. However, these breaches result from security gaps rather than from intentional attacks.

When a laptop is lost with tens of thousands or more personal details, it should be evident that the laptop user should not have been able to pull those details onto a mobile device in the first place.

Our focus in this section is on the basics of how intentional attacks take place.

There are many different methods of perpetrating cyber attacks. The one, common factor they all share is that the attackers had to find one or more gaps in a cyber system's security defenses to get in.

Cyber attackers are always looking for those vulnerabilities.

For large organizations, the megabreaches are (as previously mentioned) always retrospectively shown to have resulted from a minimum of 3 major controls either (i) failing to be present or (ii) failing to operate effectively.

Although our initial attack model is correct, the larger cyber attacks result from strategies which involve complicated, long-term battle plans. Security professionals refer to this type of strategy as the ***advanced persistent threat*** lifecycle, or ***APT*** for short:

> **advanced persistent threats (APTs)** – *a term used to describe the tenacious and highly evolved set of tactics used by hackers to infiltrate* **networks** *through* **digital devices** *and to then leave malicious software in place for as long as possible. The* **cyber attack lifecycle** *usually involves the attacker performing research & reconnaissance, preparing the most effective attack tools, getting an initial foothold into the network or target* **digital landscape***, spreading the infection and adjusting the range of attack tools in place, and then exploiting the position to maximum advantage. The purpose can be to steal, corrupt, extort and/or disrupt an organization for financial gain, brand damage or political purposes. This form of sophisticated attack becomes harder and more costly to resolve, the further into the lifecycle the attackers are and the longer the attack tools, such as malware, have managed to already remain in place. A major goal inherent in APT attacks is for the intruder to remain (persist) undetected for as long as possible in order to maximize the opportunities that result from the intrusion – for example the opportunity to steal data over a long period of time. See also* **kill-chain***.*

Perpetrators of advanced persistent threats utilize the same key cyber attack model that is at the heart of any form of cyber breach: the attackers need to find and leverage gaps in security.

The difference is that to optimize the value and the damage, the APT attackers:

- invest more time and effort into researching the target
- assemble or develop specific tools and programs to perform the initial infiltration
- seek to leverage the initial foothold to extend into more of the available territory
- remain undetected for as long as possible
- optimize their position to steal, disrupt and control as much as possible.

This type of threat is the one that major organizations which run networks and large applications fear the most. And rightly so.

The earlier in the lifecycle that any attack is detected, the cheaper and easier it is to defeat. A lot of experts look to something called the *kill chain* to help them in this effort.

The kill chain uses a list of the key steps in the advanced persistent threat lifecycle to help drive strategies and metrics to understand and improve defense.

As a proactive form of defense, the kill chain framework can help a security function to think about what it does at each step in the lifecycle to detect, deny, disrupt, disable and ultimately defeat any attack it encounters. A number of security frameworks use this model as part of their security design techniques.

As a reactive technique, each defeated attack can also record where it was in the lifecycle at the point when it was (i) detected and (ii) defeated.

This kill-chain technique does have a huge amount of value, but it also has practical problems. It works very well if all of the information of value is inside a network. However, it can easily fail to cover the security of information and systems that sit outside the network – in suppliers, cloud solutions and other locations. For many organizations, a substantial amount of the information for which they are responsible can be outside of their network.

The most critical knowledge and understanding with respect to attacks is therefore this:

> • *It is the gaps (vulnerabilities) that get targeted, not the working defenses. Don't allow the security you do have to reassure you; find out what you don't have.*

You would not be surprised to learn that, just like in the open fire door example used in Chapter 1, attackers frequently find that it is very easy to completely avoid the expensive security defenses because there is, too often, an easy and undiscovered open door that can provide the same access.

Here are a few real-world examples of how companies allow hackers to exploit security weaknesses:

• Spending millions of dollars defending an already ultra-secure cloud service but then allowing a full copy of all the information to be taken to a third party where nothing is spent on checking and implementing appropriate security.

- Creating secure applications that are so difficult to use that the intended users go rogue and use alternatives outside the network that are not monitored at all. A great example is locking down email transfers and potentially securable data transfer technologies – so users seek out exotic and unsecure alternatives.
- Creating a security architecture that only looks at items like hardware and applications and forgets to look at security requirements that can be directly embedded into the electronic information itself.

Cyber attackers are simply opportunists looking for your easiest-to-exploit gaps.

What is a Vulnerability?

A vulnerability is really any gap in security that an attacker (insider or outsider) can take advantage of.

Very often, security functions expend more effort fixing the technical vulnerabilities that they know about rather than finding the major security process gaps they do not see or understand.

A technical vulnerability can be considered to be a single deficit or absence of the right security routine or setting on a set of information, device or software application. These are important to address; just nowhere near as important as the absence of a key security process.

The large vulnerabilities occur when an important security process that should be in place is not. Process vulnerabilities tend to be the ones that lead to megabreaches.

A good way to think about this is that technical vulnerabilities can only be detected if you have a process to check for them in the first place. If you are missing a key security process, there will be clusters of technical vulnerabilities that can remain completely undetected by the organization until or unless they are compromised by a hostile party.

Think of the vulnerabilities that led to copies of emails from Mossack Fonseca – a Panama-based law firm that helps ultra-wealthy clients place their money offshore – being stolen as an example:

- The technical vulnerabilities included running out-of-date software with less-than-advisable security configuration settings.
- The process gaps that led to these vulnerabilities must have included:
  o Not running regular vulnerability assessments.
  o Not having an adequate patch and update process.
  o An unsecure record management policy (keeping years of emails live and online)
  o ...

The process gaps caused the technical gaps. Having consistent processes is the only variable that would have saved the day.

Another recent example can be seen in the 2016 Distributed Denial of Service (DDoS) attacks that leveraged quite a few different low-cost '***Internet of Things***' devices, such as digital cameras, Wi-Fi routers, and DVR players. The devices that were compromised did not have processes in place to ensure that they included basic security in their design requirements from the outset, or adequate basic security testing at any time before their commercial release. In fact, the hackers used a virus called Mirai, which scans Internet of Things devices that have factory-installed default user names and passwords, to take over these devices. This gives them a powerful army of enslaved devices (a botnet army) that can be used to overwhelm online services with data requests. In one of the Mirai incidents in 2016, this tactic was used to interrupt the Dyn company web service with cyber traffic. Dyn were themselves providing their service to help users connect with popular websites including Twitter. The resulting attack took down these services for several hours, with the attack not being defeated, but with the attackers switching it off after deciding that their point had been made.

The gap that was leveraged was a symptom that the basic security checks were not in place during design. If security people only fix that one symptom, there are likely to be further gaps that will be take advantage of – those devices need a full security review before release rather than fixes applied as they are discovered once the product is in real environments.

From any attacker's perspective, the goal is to identify and take advantage of the gaps that were forgotten.

Having a full set of security processes in place throughout the lifecycle of information and systems for which an organization is responsible helps to ensure that the technical vulnerabilities can be identified and addressed as early as possible.

Missing any critical security process creates a huge pool of open technical vulnerabilities that can be leveraged by would-be attackers.

Because vulnerabilities change over time, one of the easiest routes in for an attacker is to simply identify systems that have not been subject to regular security assessments and updates.

It is usually the failure to have these types of major processes in place (process vulnerabilities) that lead to persistent technical vulnerabilities.

The important lesson about consistency in managing vulnerabilities is this –

> • *Your largest vulnerabilities often result from failing to put essential security processes in place. Your next-largest vulnerabilities result from failing to address the critical and major gaps that the processes identify.*

Cybersecurity Principles

There are vast and complex explanations offered about cybersecurity. The basics are incredibly simple:

- The security of any electronic information you own or any digital service you rely upon has to be appropriately protected.
- That means you have to:
    1. Know about it in order to protect it.
    2. Apply appropriate safeguards and failsafes.

3. Rapidly understand any new threats and take swift action to address them.

The vast majority of organizations and individuals just do not follow these basic principles. There is even a simple checklist later on in the book (end of Chapter 9) that will allow you to check whether or not you or your organization adhere to these precepts.

Think about it:

- If systems are patched within 24 hours of an update being available
- If there is a full, single, accurate inventory of all the systems and applications used to manage information
- If systems are frequently checked to ensure they have effective security in place
- If devices have effective anti-malware installed and installation permissions removed
- If adequate encryption is running on all information of value when it is at rest or in transit

…then the risk of cyber attacks is reduced to less than 1%.

The most frequent deficit in cybersecurity is that the security function is not working from an adequately accurate or maintained information asset inventory. The clue about what creates this deficit lies in the title used to describe the Chief **Information** Security Officer. Unless the process and systems designed to capture and maintain an accurate inventory of all **information** of value to the business is in place – the security landscape will remain vulnerable.

The information locations are the supporting pillars from which all security processes are driven.

Once the information asset inventory is understood and prioritized, effective processes can feed from it to ensure that all systems and devices have security embedded by design from cradle to grave.

Although this is a very rudimentary description, it is a constant truth that having a full range of accessible, practical, easy-to-use and effective security processes in place is the driving force behind effective security.

If your security strategy is just to apply point fixes without the range of processes, then just like our security door example in Chapter 1, any motivated attacker will be able to find and get through the vulnerability equivalent of an open fire door.

> • *Fix the causes of security gaps before fixing the symptoms. There is no point in bailing water out of a boat riddled with holes. Fix key security processes and other root causes first, and then you can address the symptoms without fear of them continually returning.*

Another basic underpinning of effective security is to be sure that your security function is independently and regularly audited. I recommend annually. It is essential to ensure that the audit is truly independent and performed by a capable auditing company or auditor. If you use a vendor that has something to gain from the audit other than providing the output, or if the report goes through the security function first, then its value will be substantially diminished.

Having audited security frameworks for many years, I have noticed a strong tendency for security departments to indirectly or directly influence or offer benefits to auditing firms for providing biased or corrupted reports. It is important to ensure that audits remain independent and free from this sort of influence.

As an example, any audit company that provides other services to your company should automatically be excluded. Any use of the audit company for other services for 24 months after the audit should be similarly prohibited.

> • *Audit your security function each year through an independent party that has nothing to gain or sell from the outcome.*

More information about basic cybersecurity can be found in the chapter '**Do You Have A Megabreach Brewing?**' and also within other publications that I produce.

That chapter goes through a high-level checklist of the process gaps that indicate the cybersecurity issues have the potential to propel the organization toward a megabreach.

What Changed?

Although the fundamentals of security have remained the same (protect the information and services of value), how and where these factors are delivered has changed.

What happened was that the network stopped being the effective layer of defense that could be relied upon to prevent attacks.

Information is the new security perimeter. To be more accurate, the location of information assets has long been the foundation for informing any security function about what level of security they need to apply and where they need to apply it.

For a very long time, it was possible to apply security at an organization's network level. This would help to ensure that even if there were gaps in the security measures at other levels, the network security would act as a reliable defensive safety net.

That is no longer true.

All organizations now depend on suppliers, cloud services, mobile devices and other locations that operate outside of their network. Some of these information assets (assets for which the organization still has responsibility) never even enter the organization's network.

Added to this, even within the network, the security measures no longer offer 100% resilience, not even close.

The growth in the amount and sophistication of malware, coupled with the increased speed of network communications, means that most networks exist in a '***clopen***' state. That is to say that even though you may intend for your network to be closed off from external threats, the reality is that security functions are engaged in constant cat and mouse games of identifying and eliminating intrusions.

What this means is that *how* we achieve security has changed, but the security objectives have not.

A major problem during the transition of security from network-centric to information-centric is that most security experts are used to running a network-centric model.

Legacy experts got used to being able to treat the network security level as a safety net. It was also more cost-effective to apply security at the network level. If people did stupid things within the network, these mistakes were rarely likely to lead to significant problems or losses.

Security experts were trained to understand the path rather than the destination. To save money, security managers were often required to minimize (or ignore) the need to embed security directly in information and applications and instead relied on network security measures to provide a cost-effective safety net.

Then changes in technology created two huge shifts:

- The network was no longer an adequate security shield.
- PLUS - many of the critical services moved out of the network

While security still has to secure the critical information, services and devices that are required for each organization to be able to do business, these shifts forced the path to achieving those objectives to change.

But even those organizations that have responded correctly to these shifts by implementing new security processes have experienced difficulties. I have seen these issues emerging on jobs in which I have been sent in to look at bleeding edge technologies by companies that take the right approach, as well as on jobs where the organization knows they have security gaps.

The gaps are always a result of this shift. If a new technology is required by an organization, the right approach is for the security function to assess it from the very beginning – and to also determine if a new process is required because the business is expected to make additional, similar requests in the future.

However, what frequently happens is that the new technology is so unknown that the security function fails to engage with it. They either exclude it from their remit, or try to handle it through nebulous guidance, such as just referring to generic, one-size-fits-all security principles rather than generating assistance specific to the need.

Obtaining a new cloud or supplier service?

Where critical information is involved, an effective security service will develop architecture standards and insist that these standards must be included in the supplier contract. The security department will also verify controls before the service goes live, have escalation processes for any non-standard features or queries and also include a requirement to re-check the security on a defined and regular basis.

An ineffective security function will just throw a one-size-fits-all contract at it and may not even check that the measures are in place before the service goes live.

Since technologies now change so fast, an effective security function is one that assesses and defines appropriate new security services to ensure security is always included by design.

Failing to rapidly meet the security needs of new technology from the outset also results in people and groups within an organization doing their own thing without adequate guidance.

Unsanctioned use of technology is now frequently referred to as the new '*Shadow IT*'. This term used to refer to groups spending money to create technology that intentionally bypassed security processes.

Now, however, shadow IT is found much more frequently in organizations where the security department has limited or no capability to provide their users with the security processes that allow these users to quickly and safely select and use new technologies.

If a person wants to use a new type of presentation software, telling him or her that it is unsupported or unsecure without offering adequate information or alternatives promotes unsanctioned use.

Similarly, blocking major cloud services leads to employees and other company associates finding even worse workarounds:

- Leaving the corporate network to gain access without going through the usual defense layers.
- Seeking alternative technologies that are less well known and probably have much greater security issues.

So what has changed is that security is no longer about supporting internal technologies and focusing on securing the network layer. Certainly these are still important – but when securing the information layer, if security processes to manage new and external technologies are not an embedded part of the processes – there will be open vulnerabilities aplenty, offering cyber attackers a healthy set of options to take advantage of.

Assessing the Threat Landscape

Whether or not you fall victim to a major attack will depend a lot on what your threat landscape looks like. For each organization, the threat landscape is different and depends on a number of factors.

An easy way to think about this is to use the HAGS acronym:

- **H**istory – does your organization already have a track record of being compromised?
- **A**ctivities – Does what you do involve transacting a lot of money or high-value information or performing tasks that can be controversial and provoke activists – and their cyber counterparts – the hacktivists?
- **G**aps – Do you have a clear picture of how significant the gaps in your security are? The more gaps you have, the more at risk you are. If you don't have a clear picture of your gaps for critical information and services, then your risk level is undoubtedly somewhere off the charts.
- **S**cale – the larger your organization is and the more people who use and access its cyber systems, the greater the risk.

Small organizations, handling low-value information, delivering non-controversial services with reasonable security are clearly much safer than organizations at the other end of the spectrum are.

Cybersecurity Summarized

Ad-hoc and network-centric methods of controlling cybersecurity are no longer effective.

What does work in today's cyber environment is to have a comprehensive set of efficient security processes that cover the full lifecycle of all the critical electronic information and digital services on which an organization relies.

Where the information of value is permitted to go defines where the security and security processes are required.

Effective processes ensure that the footprint of that information can be actively regulated, secured and controlled throughout its lifecycle.

All of the business's control decisions come from the business using the processes – and the security function is responsible for keeping those processes up to date and relevant.

Yes – technical security vulnerabilities need to be addressed. However, without full process coverage, an organization will find itself in the same position as the company with the expensive fire door, referred to in Chapter 1. The attackers will not waste their time trying to defeat the high security measures on one wall if the other is wide open.

It is easy to identify the few companies that run security well. They have great, clear and easy-to-access security processes. The staff within their organizations feels that security is an efficient enabler that allows them to adopt and use new technologies with appropriate safeguards.

Organizations that do not achieve these goals are deteriorating quickly.

4: Security Psychology and The Medusa Effect

Psychology, Meet Technology

'It's not identifying all of the security gaps that will be the problem.'

I looked around the room. The interview was supposed to be a one-on-one, but turned out to be a meeting with an executive team of eight people.

They knew their security position had some deficits.

One by one they had asked their questions. I love my subject. One by one I had very carefully and succinctly answered them.

All the people in the room were looking at each other with a mixture of hope and something approaching excitement. All of them except one person, that is. He was looking at his shoes and nodding his head like this would be yet another avenue to failure.

'Identifying how to fix the technical and process problems is also relatively simple,' I continued. 'The problem that is hardest to overcome is getting the endorsement required to fix the gaps.'

They did not believe me. They were so pleased to have found someone who could unpack and answer their security issues, they felt that would be enough.

I left the room with that impression.

I was already under offer from a major bank to help design their cybersecurity architecture, but this assignment involved what was for me the more familiar territory of diagnosing, planning and fixing an entire security function.

My partner asked me how it went. 'Really well,' I said. And then, I incorrectly assessed the opinion of the man who had been staring at his shoes. 'Apart from one person,' I added. 'He seemed to think that I wasn't going to be able to work out the gaps and fixes required.'

In fact, that one guy – let's call him 'Bob' – thought nothing of the kind. What Bob thought was that I was going to do the usual security two-step. He thought I would come on board, find out how bad things were and then join in with the group denial.

In fact, 'Bob' is the one person from that meeting who I still see occasionally.

It would turn out that quite a few people already knew what was wrong – and how to fix it. They were just not being listened to.

Before we continue with this story, we need to consider some psychological phenomena. These are really important factors that tend to affect board members and security managers.

If you want to make a difference, whether as an executive decision maker or as a security manager, it is important to understand certain human psychological responses to challenging situations:

1) **The Comfort Zone**. We all have a comfort zone. If something pushes anyone too far outside his or her comfort zone, that person will do just about *anything* to get back inside it.
2) **Group Denial**. This is a classic response to a traumatic circumstance. If you present a group with a wall of fact-based evidence that creates a potentially career-devastating risk that has a relatively high probability of happening, but a small probability of not happening immediately, the group will find any way it can to marginalize and bury the information.
3) **Bias**. Since peoples' beliefs are shaped more by their past knowledge and present position than by immediate fact-based evidence with which they are presented, this introduces an inherent bias against the new evidence. This factor is especially relevant to security management.

You might think that if you present clear information about security risk, with concise supporting evidence and a clear action plan, it will be endorsed, but this doesn't happen, largely because of these psychological factors.

The challenge is that the situation that gets outlined can very easily push all three of the psychological red buttons listed above – and this will lead the recipients of the information to interpret it like this:

- The level of risk and the required actions are far outside our comfort zone.
- It is safer to deny the new reality that is being pushed than to accept and deal with it.
- Either our knowledge and perceptions are so wrong that abandoning them will place us in personal jeopardy, OR the presenter is wrong and needs to be marginalized.

> - *If you have security risk information that is going to be way outside a group's comfort zone, you have to present it in stages, with solutions that form a comfortable trail. Only if you allow your audience's comfort zone to gradually change to the point that they can cope with the information will they be able to accept it.*

Sometimes, however, the situation is so bad, you may not have the time to adjust the recipient's comfort zone.

However, a choice to present an overwhelming situation to people who would need to deal with the actions and consequences invokes a phenomenon I like to refer to as the Medusa effect…

The Medusa Effect

Rapidly unveiling a devastating security status to an executive audience will cause them to look immediately in any other direction for fear of being mortally wounded by examining the facts. This is usually followed by some form of immediate exile or marginalization for the presenter.

Getting any person, let alone a group of executives, to acknowledge and deal with the current rate of technological change is like asking them to stare into the face of Medusa (the mythical being that destroyed people by turning them into stone). Very few people are willing to stare directly at the rapid changes.

Disclosing and evidencing the impact that the rate of change has on the security vulnerability for any organization that has significant gaps amplifies the Medusa effect.

Any security professional who really knows his or her stuff also knows that taking the raw facts about a weak security position into a room of senior decision-makers and unveiling it can feel like asking them to accept the end of their own lives. The individuals in the group receiving the information will mostly look anywhere else to avoid looking directly at the problems. They will find an excuse to seek the safest route out of the room and will seek reassurance in their collective desire to deny the situation.

As a last resort, it is possible to directly communicate the overwhelming information; however, that tends to result in behaviors and outcomes that in almost all circumstances are undesirable. Specifically – the underlying problems will not be addressed and the subsequent actions from the executive will be geared towards marginalizing the risk for themselves. They will not prioritize the long-term needs and sustainability of the organization above their own immediate futures.

If you are asking yourself this question: 'Can the security position be fixed without substantially affecting the status quo?' – the answer is that it can be handled reasonably sensitively – but there are usually some significant changes required. Often this includes an initial substantial uplift in budget, a reprioritization of actions, together with re-focusing and re-training many of the security people.

It is achievable – but it is not easy.

The fact that most senior executives know that their organization has security issues to overcome should not be misunderstood. . They simply fear the pain, cost, risk and consequences of endorsing the large changes required more than they fear remaining with the current risk.

Just because something is correct and can be fully evidenced does not mean it will be accepted. Far from it.

Executives are not stupid; they are highly intelligent, politically savvy and financially oriented. Their contracts are not (at present) geared towards any long-term consequences for their short-term actions and decisions. Even if they have shareholding interests, it can seem more beneficial for them to bury the risk and tie up their financial interests than to face down the consequences and cost of resolving deep-rooted security rot.

Corporate politics, personal careers and immediate financial implications will take precedence over facts. All of these factors need to be carefully considered and navigated.

If you present the evidence and situation to a manager without using all of the right soft skills (adjusting the comfort zone, navigating the politics and communicating well), expect the following:

If you are junior enough, they may just sideline you as a neurotic troublemaker.

If you are senior enough, they will look to change your assignment or shuffle you out.

Consider what happened when Yahoo did the right thing by identifying and fixing their security issues. They lost a major takeover deal, lost about 20% of their immediate company value ($1 billion) and instead of being praised for finding and addressing a problem – they were lambasted for allowing the issues to occur in the first place.

When Yahoo sought to fix their security and uncovered one of the largest breaches in history, the executives in charge, including the CISO who had only taken on the role in late 2015, were not rewarded, the customers did not thank them, and the immediate damage was substantial. A major wound was revealed and everybody, including the cyber criminals, initially treated the organization much worse than they would have if Yahoo had allowed the wound to continue to be buried.

It also came to light, in late 2016, that Yahoo had been breached twice in the past. An earlier breach in 2013 had exposed 1 billion customer credentials, twice the number involved in the breach that had been identified as occurring 'some time' in late 2014.

So to avoid the Medusa effect, as part of an organization's mitigation strategy, it is vital to consider this cyber house rule:

> • *If you are riddled with intruders, don't expect to just push them out or they will attempt to destroy you.*

Intelligent CISOs are well aware of this fact. Indeed, it is a result of the way that the advanced persistent threat cyber attack lifecycle operates, as covered earlier in the book.

Consider:

- Most organizations are riddled with cybersecurity gaps.
- That means their systems are infested with malware that the attackers conceal because it financially benefits them to remain undetected.
- Once the organization starts closing down the malware, the cyber criminal's monetization route changes. He or she no longer needs to keep quiet. Instead, the criminal(s) now need to conduct a fire sale of all the information they have on that organization.

Think about it. The Yahoo data had been taken around 2 and 3 years before it was disclosed. The only thing that changed is that Yahoo took the steps to improve their security approach, including improved disclosure transparency.

A CISO new to an organization who discovers that vast changes are required will personally be much better off moving on. This is one of the factors influencing the fact that the average time in a CISO role is 17 months. The CISOs who move on do so for one of two main reasons. They either tried unsuccessfully to gain support to address the issues, triggered the Medusa effect, and were pushed out, or they saw how inflexible the political situation was and decided to move to an organization with a more manageable or recoverable security position.

Skilled CISOs who really know what they are doing are in limited supply, and can pick and chose where they work.

Conversely, a CISO who joins in with the denial of the situation can often ride along with burying the risk until or unless a devastating breach occurs.

This might sound like burying security risk is the best idea. Unfortunately, this is a short and medium-term strategy adopted by many, and is one of the main contributing factors to megabreaches continuing to surface and surprise organizations.

It is not an effective long-term strategy. Hiding and avoiding critical and major security risks has devastating long-term effects.

In November 2016, a UK supermarket bank, Tesco Bank, was hit by a major hack. The cyber criminals got deeply into the bank's systems and managed to complete fraudulent transactions on some 9,000 customer accounts. Small banks (Tesco only had 136,000 regular checking accounts) may believe robust security systems are beyond their means, but this is untrue. They can recover from breaches and get great security – but the odds are against them. Both existing customers and potential new customers alike lost confidence in the bank's security after the breach occurred.

If the bank can prove that the attack was exceptional and was not due to a list of internal security shortcomings, the trust can be restored. However, as we know – any megabreach like this will turn out to result from 3 or more critical and major security gaps.

In the weeks following the Tesco attack, it turned out that many different security organizations had been raising alerts to them about their substantial security gaps. There were – guess what – more than three of them.

One of the most bizarre observations about the Tesco Bank attack was that it *unexpectedly* happened over a weekend when security and staffing were at their lowest. Any cyber criminal knows that holidays and weekends are absolutely the best time to perform a cyber heist.

Christmas Day, New Years Day, Thanksgiving or most weekends are best for cyber theft attacks. Working days are best for ransom demands and interruptions of business activities.

So – how did the list of security issues at Tesco remain neglected and unfixed? Were executives notified about the security gaps, and did they ignore these warnings? Was the security function prevented from bringing the gaps to the company executives' attention?

Whether this breach stemmed from negligence on the part of the security function or the executives, either scenario is endemic in countless organizations. A vast number of major organizations know that they have large numbers of security gaps. However, that information is often suppressed below the board level – and even when it is mentioned to the board, the security function tends to do this after informing board members that living with these gaps is a usual practice.

After all, the incorrect consensus sold to most executive boards is that any major organization cannot prevent megabreaches.

The truth is that some security compromises cannot be prevented, but **a megabreach requires a preventable chain of critical gaps to coexist.**

It might be that a brand new type of cyber attack (a **zero-day** attack) can create a critical vulnerability for a short time. However, a single critical vulnerability on its own has never been the sole cause of a megabreach.

In another of my books (*Cybersecurity for Beginners*) – I refer to this as '**stacked risk**' – where a chain of sometimes seemingly unrelated security gaps come together to form a much greater risk than their individual components suggest would be possible.

Looking individually at security risks, silo by silo, gives a false impression about the true risk picture.

Consider the Target megabreach back in 2013, in which there were a list of major security controls that, had any one of them functioned, would have prevented the event. The successful attack required that all of those gaps aligned to create a path for the theft of millions of customers' credit and debit card details.

Likewise, at Mossack Fonseca, there was a long list of major and critical gaps, including out-of-date software, poor security configuration and bad record management (keeping over a decade's worth of email open to Internet access).

A key contributor to preventing these security gaps from being fixed is revealed by understanding what motivates the decision makers, due to the fact that employment contracts are all designed around short-term success.

> • *Always remember: employees do what optimizes their personal objectives and that can be (1) in conflict with the organization's objectives and (2) manipulated unless the right rules and consequences are in place. For example – people managing critical infrastructure systems are making decisions that can lead to loss of life with almost no fear of personal reprisals for getting it wrong.*

People are naturally motivated and biased toward information and decisions that support the most beneficial personal outcome. Since they are almost always paid monthly, the short-term outcome is most important, and, in addition, being confronted with any possibly adverse impact on their immediate personal situation has exactly the opposite effect – it leads to bias against the information and decisions that threaten them.

Even when the consequences of ignoring something can create devastating long-term harm, it is rare that an individual will make choices which will create *definite*, near-immediate personal financial harm simply to prevent the *probability* of a massive future impact to others.

This can be seen with certain choices made about critical national infrastructure.

• On the one side, various governments like those in the United States and UK are directing organizations to avoid certain hardware brands (such as certain devices and microchips manufactured by companies with partial Chinese ownership) that have in the past been found to have built-in security issues. Those issues are alleged to be due to adversarial nation state involvement by China and others in the ownership and management of those hardware companies. More specifically, it is believed that much of this hardware includes backdoors and remote operation capabilities that could be used to launch a cyber attack – a secret endemic invasion that could be switched on.

- On the other side, the same governments tend to go and do exactly what they are telling others not to. They will and have endorsed entire nuclear power stations like the one at Hinkley Point in the UK, which will be financed by those same nation states they consider to be adversarial and untrustworthy.

The near-term financial benefits overrule the long-term risk considerations unless this mindset undergoes changes supported by decision-makers at the very top.

Unless responsibilities for the long-term consequences are built into decision making powers, decisions favor the short-term outcomes regardless of the long-term consequences.

If I were hiring a CISO, I would require that the employment contract contained a personal liability clause for any decisions this person made to extend for many years into the future, in light of this proposal:

If you fail to recommend and implement adequate security provisions that could reasonably be expected, and if this gap causes or substantially contributes to a major disruption or loss of business, your personal liability will translate into your annual earnings for each year in which such a mistake was made.

You may think this is harsh. It is, but it is also really effective. No security manager with this clause will sit quietly on anything that needs to be done. Nobody who doubts his or her ability to perform the job competently will consider taking it on.

A similar security clause is then also contractually needed at the executive board level.

Realistically, few organizations would consider doing this. That is unfortunate, because it really would positively change the security dynamics.

Consequences motivate people to make the right security decisions, at the right time and based on the right information.

Overcoming the Medusa effect in any of the majority of organizations with deep-set security issues requires the CISO and the CEO to agree to change the executive mindset.

> • *Executive dynamics result in security function heads being incentivized by boards to bury risks more often than they are encouraged to resolve them. An effective CISO has to change that dynamic through soft skills (planning, communication and political maneuvering).*

As outlined in the above cyber house rule, overcoming the challenge is reliant on a robust set of soft skills: planning, communication and political maneuvering.

Planning means not just operationally addressing the technical and process security gaps – but also gradually bringing about the executive understanding and endorsement in the first place.

If I want to marry someone, I don't ask them for that commitment on a first date and expect to be successful. I need to spend time developing the relationship. To bring about change, the effective CISO has to do the same thing. He or she has to plan how to rapidly, but incrementally, bring about the changes required by first gaining the trust and confidence of the executive.

Communication is key to bringing about these changes. Too much too soon brings about the negative behaviors typical of the response to being dragged too quickly outside one's comfort zone – internal abandonment and sabotage.

Too little communication and the security function looks incompetent. Achieving the right amount of communication is like laying a perfect trail of breadcrumbs. If you get your security communications right, your department will be seen as one that enables a brighter, bigger and more sustainable future.

Transforming any organization with deep-set security issues is very achievable. Robust security is both possible and creates enormous competitive advantages and opportunities. When executives buy into this, it is possible to persuade them to do the right thing and support the right decisions.

> • *Executives invest in what they prefer, not what they need. Your job is to get them to prefer what they need.*

Part of persuading the executive requires understanding and navigating all the relevant internal political positions. This is the hardest part and is often where many (including myself) sometimes choose to throw in the towel!

How Boardroom Denial Operates

One of the reasons I was encouraged to write this book was to help eliminate the myth that good security is on an unreachable plane of existence.

Give me the organization and I can find the gaps and provide the solutions. The challenge is that for many organizations, just comprehending the gaps creates a traumatic situation.

In any major organization, to get to a position where these gaps appeared and grew would have taken a number of people and decisions. It is most often those same people who are then asked to stare directly at the deficits they believe they created and to agree to present what can appear to be their own incompetence to their employers or shareholders.

Having or facing up to security gaps does not reflect incompetence. Hostile parties are finding new ways to create security gaps all the time. Something could have been a perfectly valid approach 3 years ago – but may be in urgent need of repair or replacement now. The incompetence lies in leaving those gaps open. However, as outlined in this chapter, if you bring the information straight to an executive – this is what can easily happen…

You may recall that interview from earlier in the chapter. Later the same day, I received a call with a contract offer and a request to start the assignment as soon as possible.I accepted the offer and started just a few days later.

On day one, more of the political situation was revealed to me. There was an existing department that my role and title superseded. The executives suspected that the people in the existing department were not all that competent, but I was given assurances of transparency and support.

The existing department provided no support or assistance and was as defensive as possible about any information or access relating to the organization's cybersecurity status. They did everything possible to hide everything, especially the gaps they did know about.

However, I did have some people assigned directly to me that also had an indirect reporting relationship to that business security group.

As a seasoned professional security manager with an extensive background in security auditing, I can fortunately work backwards through any evidence. That is, I can look at symptoms and understand which controls and process gaps had to be in place for them to be present.

Until this particular assignment, twelve was the highest number of critical and major security gaps I had found in any single organization's digital landscape. I was close to that number by the end of day one, and by the end of week one, I was up in the twenties.

I have a dashboard I use that is closely aligned with ISACA COBIT (control objectives for information and related technology) and other leading security frameworks. My dashboard was a wall of red, with very occasional yellow.

One by one, I identified the missing factors, collected the evidence, identified the impact and also started to formulate the remediation strategy. It was all fixable but there was a lot to do.

The business managers were frustrated with processes from the existing security department that were resulting in impractical working conditions. As an example, the marketing department had to go to the local coffee shop or work from home in order to access critical assets such as their Facebook accounts. (They had blocked Facebook access for everyone within the network.)

It was a master class in how to manage security ineffectively.

Less than one percent of the servers they used had anti-malware. Their file transfers from outside the network went directly into the network before they were scanned for any malware. A vast amount of sensitive information was stored, unencrypted, in file shares that hundreds of administrators could access. Just about every system had unique identity and access controls. Any security professional knows that the more identity and access systems you use, the greater the chances that people will be able to achieve or retain unauthorized access, simply because there are too many access points to monitor.

At this point, it is worth stating that this was the worst set of security circumstances I had ever seen. They had practically nothing to sustain security except for quite a loyal and dedicated staff.

In fact, what I listed above was less than 20% of what I found.

They had recently implemented a very rudimentary ***data loss prevention*** (DLP) tool. It was triggering alerts like crazy. The existing security team was busy mopping up the symptoms of the incidents without addressing the root causes and thought this was a success.

Data Loss Prevention should always be considered a last line of defense. If you fail to have the right security in layers where it should have been present, DLP technology is useful to help identify that you have deeper issues.

If my DLP finds that an employee is trying to send out or store 10,000 customer credit card details, I should be understanding and fixing how they got to access and collect that many details from the systems in the first place. The security should have been effective far sooner than at the very last moment when the crime or exploit could have been successful.

> • *The extent to which your last lines of cyber defense get triggered and used (for example - recovery management and information loss prevention alerts) is an effective measure of how many gaps you have in your primary security defenses.*

A number of internal parties were rapidly waking up to just how bad the security position was.

Their existing security function still believed that their anti-malware (of that time) was still able to receive updates for new malware overnight that would combat the latest threats. But even then, they had not implemented it on almost all of their servers.

The waves of the Medusa effect were already taking hold. The promised support was taking impossible waves of political heat to re-manage the situation. With less than two weeks in place, I knew that the best I was capable of achieving was to ensure that the organization had an informed view of their position.

They liked my ability to identify the risks and actions but were overwhelmed by the implications.

'We can't present this; we will all look like (flaming) idiots,' stated one executive – except the word he used was not flaming.

So I did what so many other good security professionals do. I declined the opportunity to sit quietly on the megabreach waiting to be discovered and moved on to a role that paid better.

'Bob' was amazed. He never expected that.

I provided my report, with evidence, and it was quietly filed away and ignored.

There were a couple of really great security professionals in place who understood the severity of the situation and stayed to try to correct it. They are no longer at that company. The people who buried the risk and managed the security are still there. I have no idea how much was ever fixed.

If you think this situation is rare, you only need to look at every single megabreach for another example of exactly the same thing.

Companies receive large numbers of warnings about their security gaps that they ignore or inadequately follow up. Leaving those issues in place inevitably culminates in a megabreach.

Naturally, not every organization with these kinds of gaps has already had a megabreach. That factor (no megabreach yet) is the one that can sustain security at an unacceptably low level. People can do a really bad job of managing security and remain in place until a megabreach occurs.

It is easy to tell if you are that type of organization – just head to the chapter on 'Do You Have a Megabreach Brewing?' and you can use the information there to work it out, even if you are not in the security department.

It is also really important to understand that all of this does not mean that there are not plenty of highly skilled security professionals out there. Most people, even in the organization I used as an example, were doing their specific jobs very well.

Most security professionals I meet are excellent at what they do.

The challenge is primarily driven by the paradigm change. The way security needs to be managed has changed and the most senior security professionals are seldom motivated to learn about and then implement what is required. Their immediate personal circumstances are best served by burying the risks.

'Bob' shrewdly thought that if I wanted a future in his organization, my best bet would have been to join in on the group denial...

I reflected on that point as I sat in on a meeting. An organization with security gaps you could fly a 747 through convened a meeting of senior staff to look at a really tiny technical security deficit in an unreleased web platform. At the end of the meeting, I was instructed not to raise a risk report about the really large problems.

The next time someone alerts you to a security gap, just remember this:

> • *If you shoot the messengers, for some reason, they stop bringing you information.*

If you motivate your security function correctly, they will provide what you need. If you feel more comfortable denying the risk, you may survive in the short term.

In a company that encourages security staff to bury security risk, even if that motivation is accidental, the security position will threaten the future of the organization. It is only a matter of time until they encounter their megabreach and its consequences.

5: Yesterday's Security Tomorrow

Although the objectives for security have remained the same, the path to achieving effective security has changed.

It used to be the case that information resided exclusively inside networks and malware threats could easily be automatically detected and eliminated on all the devices (the endpoints) used.

Heavy investment in network and endpoint security could be relied upon to prevent most security threats from being realized.

It was still important to apply appropriate security on critical applications, such as those that managed financial transactions. However, there was little to no chance that a security intrusion could exist and persist throughout the network, monitoring, stealing or disrupting transactions.

The biggest threats under the old system came from one or more insiders colluding to steal data or to perform unauthorized transactions through legitimate accounts.

Now, the digital ecosystem extends far beyond the network perimeter, and most of the network and endpoint (device) level security can easily be circumvented by attackers.

The new digital ecosystem has created new vulnerabilities, which, in turn, have led to new threats. The result is that network and endpoint security inside an organization no longer form the security safety net that they once did. The footprint of the digital ecosystem now extends well beyond the traditional network security perimeter.

Despite this, security functions continue to spend disproportionate amounts of time and money on trying to fix the vulnerabilities relating to the network perimeter layer, without adequate attention to the vulnerability layers that arise from organizations' reliance on outside cloud providers and subcontractors, without realizing that fixing the latter vulnerabilities can make the more profound difference.

Existing security frameworks, such as the excellent ISACA COBIT, correctly identify what needs to be achieved. However, budget limitations and the practicality of what used to work led most security functions to take shortcuts in the past and to continue to do so at the present time.

Security functions did not routinely enforce a manageable, single identity and access architecture since they often considered this to be uneconomical. Financial limitations also led these legacy security functions to focus on placing security only on the internal applications directly under their control.

But as malware became better at bypassing security, applications based on cloud and supplier systems were increasingly adopted to transact critical information, and mobile devices became more widely used than traditional PC operating systems, most security functions failed to update their focus and methods to meet these changing conditions. Those which failed to embed the necessary security principles found themselves, and continue to find themselves, wide open to attack.

Upgrading security to address those gaps requires two things:

1) Going back to the basic objectives and putting security in place on all the layers where it can and should exist.
2) Paying special attention to all new technologies and digital services on which information of value will be placed in the future or is already transacted.

Security functions in organizations not used to doing this struggle to achieve these goals because it requires a wholesale change in how they manage security.

It is difficult to translate the existing security frameworks into the specific implementation steps required, especially if the security function has never seen the correct approach in action.

The result is that these security functions revert to doing what they have always done. They look to upgrade security inside networks and existing internal technologies rather than facing the steep learning curve required to take their entire security architecture to a new level that encompasses deploying security at all possible layers.

There are logical and easy security steps that can be taken to vastly improve security, yet the expert decision makers have a tendency to ignore these steps and to deploy what is familiar to them.

This bias is not restricted to major organizations.

Here is a great example. Late in 2016, the UK government set aside $2.3 billion to enhance the country's cybersecurity.

Instead of formulating a truly effective master plan, what immediately happened was that government officials adopted low value, barely effective initiatives and put them in place across government departments.

For a fraction of the money, they could have rapidly put 99.7% effective artificial intelligence anti-malware across all government systems within a few months. Instead, one of their high-priority initiatives involved mandating the deployment of email filters to block obvious spam and to reduce some of the really basic phishing attacks, leaving the more sophisticated phishing attacks working just fine.

Not only was this really poor value for the money, but this technique almost always causes interruptions to operations when legitimate emails that don't meet the standards are also blocked. It also encourages new security risks as employees find workarounds through unguarded channels (such as webmail) so they can continue to transact what they need.

On the upside, the individuals who did not make the right decisions earned some great money with no future consequences.

> - *Guidance on security is rarely challenged. If you pay someone to give you security guidance, he or she will give you an answer with conviction, but it may not be correct or up to date. Verify that security guidance is up to date and valid before relying upon it.*

With a really sound master plan, the national security initiative could transform security by correctly evaluating and prioritizing the actions with the most security impact, with much lower operational impact.

As another example, the UK has laws that (inadvisably) allow huge amounts of resident data into the public and global domain. The inadvisability of this practice is exemplified by a test given to first graders in the US, which correctly educates young children not to put full name, address and other personal data online. Conversely, UK laws require a substantial amount of personal data to be publically available. This practice has devastating consequences for private individuals and companies alike; it gives identity thieves and other types of thieves easier access to extort peoples' money and other assets.

It is completely understandable that government agencies may need open access to personal information – but putting it on the Internet and continuing to keep it there? Truly dumb.

This is a great example of yesterday's security tomorrow.

The security function can pick away at familiar, incremental and low-value security activities. They will be able to prove that their actions make a difference, but the government's officials or the organization's executives will not understand that the security department is not addressing the issues that really need to be resolved to improve security.

For the same budget, the UK government initiative could have implemented actions that would have made the UK and its government systems a really hard target for cyber attacks.

They could, for example, have almost fully eliminated successful phishing attacks without interrupting operations, by spending little more than they did to implement email controls that only reduced a small percentage of the least-sophisticated phishing attempts.

This is not only happening to nation states; major organizations and small businesses are suffering in the same ways.

My review, assessment, and comments on a major organization's security upgrade efforts show how an outdated and shortsighted approach can lead any type of business or other organization into a similar downhill spiral. This was my assessment:

This organization was investing substantial funds to upgrade their security, but their plans were focused on the ad-hoc items with which they were familiar, and had delivery timescales that were going to be outpaced by the threats they faced.

Instead of creating a master plan that encompassed their full digital ecosystem, addressed the root causes and properly fixed all the necessary processes, they planned to provide partial fixes that mostly mopped up symptoms.

Their superficial bandaid plan contained no provisions to upgrade to an over-arching security architecture, with coverage beyond the internal network into cloud, supplier and customer systems.

Most of their budget was allocated for internal network items that should have been in place 5 years ago, but under their proposal, would not even become fully operational for another 2 years.

Worse still, some of their planned 'upgrades' had the potential to build in new security vulnerabilities that could enable a skilled hacker to bring their entire multi-billion dollar empire to a standstill. These supposed upgrades included some security technologies that would entail putting master switches in place that could easily bring every internal system to a grinding halt if a cyber attacker could gain access or if any legitimate, approved user implemented the wrong settings.

This plan was focused almost exclusively on items within their network. Once the network perimeter was reached, the plans screeched to a halt and contained only a one-size-fits-all contract with a woefully inadequate, ineffective and inefficient reactive assessment schedule.

I recommended a revised plan that would allow the company to build in security by design, which in turn would allow them to rapidly transition to having a fully-secure digital ecosystem. The budget requirements were no different than those for their original plans, but the necessary actions and activities were completely divergent.

If you are interested, the plan I provided is broadly outlined in the next chapter.

It was not a risky plan. It had already been implemented and was in operation at several competitors' organizations. It would, however, make a big difference and would work very quickly. It would also enable (through processes) any of their business functions to elevate their legacy systems to a strong level of security much faster than the mop-up plan would have done.

I provided an example:

- This particular organization had been deploying systems and applications with low, medium and high security requirements onto any spare infrastructure they had. The result was that they could not isolate and protect systems of different value without disentangling the mess.
- If instead they fixed the deployment process so that all future deployments are zoned onto appropriate low, medium or high security infrastructure, the problem would be permanently resolved. All they would need to do is redeploy any critical applications. All new applications would be deployed into appropriate network and server areas.

Their plan was only to look at disentangling some of the high value systems – and to do that without even establishing a single, authoritative and accurate inventory of those systems in the first place.

So did they continue with their plan or adopt the proposal that I demonstrated would work better?

They stuck with their existing plan. The security function existed without adequate auditing or accountability – and the last thing they wanted to do was to radically change their approach.

> - *If you get the security team to score their own performance, don't expect full transparency and an honest result.*

My plan ventured into unfamiliar territory for this security team. It would involve substantial changes to how they operated and require what was considered to be difficult political negotiation with other departments.

Even though many security departments refuse to shake themselves up by changing their mindset and operations, some do venture outside their comfort zone and discover that it is actually possible to have secure systems.

It is also true that if you are operating those systems over public channels like the Internet, there will be some minor compromises. However, with the right security embedded by design, those compromises will never be of megabreach proportions.

Although it is now essential for organizations to detect and recover from those minor compromises, the vast majority of the intrusions that are discovered are preventable.

These gaps persist because the way that security needs to be run has changed, but often the actual working practices that underlie these changes have not.

It is not possible for major organizations to protect against megabreaches without having a well-thought-through master plan that embeds appropriate security consistently across the digital ecosystem.

Most security is running at least 3 years behind where it needs to be. Most (but not all) organizations are running initiatives that plan to eventually put in place embedded security processes that should have been designed into the original digital ecosystem many years ago.

As long as security teams continue to play catch-up at this slow pace, the rate of cybercrime will continue to grow.

The best security managers are evolving their approach from network security into a more comprehensive agile cybersecurity model that spans outside the network and considers how to embed security appropriately into every component and layer.

However, if you look at security expenditures and at breach patterns, this evolution is happening too slowly. A disproportionate amount of effort is still spent on legacy concepts that can no longer provide a safety net.

Multiple factors push security management to deal with the changes incrementally, rather than stepping back and revising their approach more holistically. Incremental security changes are encouraged by these factors:

- The available security frameworks that guide security planning and implementation have always lagged some 2 to 3 years behind the current needs. This used to be an acceptable norm.
- As covered in the previous chapter, even when a security manager knows what to do, gaining executive endorsement for the enormous required changes is difficult.
- Many existing security teams are trained for legacy activities that often do not meet the organization's current needs; this undermines the security manager's need for a strong and supportive team.

All of this means that the security improvements taking place are often inefficiently focused.

On the one hand, there are brand new security technologies, such as artificial intelligence based anti-malware with 99% plus endpoint effectiveness – and on the other are the legacy anti-virus solutions with approaches that are far less effective.

If your company already has a multi-year pricing deal in place for a security technology that has passed its expiration date – what do you do? If you suggest buying new technology, this can undermine the earlier decision to buy the previous solution.

In fact, there are so many costly new and updated security solutions that many decisions about upgrading are marketing-led and are reinforced by legacy contractual and employment commitments rather than by their true value.

When you have teams of internal network staff and legions of network security devices with expensive legacy device contracts, there is a propensity to favor updated versions of what you have rather than looking to change what you buy and use.

Most often, decisions about whether or not to change up to more effective technologies and new skills are passed down to those who will be most negatively impacted by them.

Ask a security department if they want to be audited – and they will likely find a way to come up with reasons against it.

Ask a network security team if they would like to change to a process that eliminates most of their workload and you find the same thing.

> • *Do not ask the turkeys to vote for Christmas. Leaving security decisions for creation and approval through the people it will negatively impact will not generate the required outcomes. People with the wrong skills and domain knowledge will not vote to replace themselves.*

Remember, to escape from deploying yesterday's security tomorrow, informed decisions must be made independently, not by people who are impacted by these decisions.

Security Frameworks Need to Get Agile

There are plenty of effective security frameworks out there. These are sets of objectives or explicit controls that help to ensure security is implemented effectively.

Examples of these frameworks include ISACA COBIT, ISO 2700x, COSO, NIST and the Payment Card Industry Data Security Standards (PCI DSS).

They all do a good job of articulating the basic requirements.

However, in the past, security frameworks were able to operate with lifecycles that spanned several years. A new security technique or process would come into existence. After a few years, it would become an established practice. At that point it would be included in newer versions of the security framework.

This led organizations using the updated frameworks to not implement important new security controls until a few years after they were actually needed.

This endangered the organization's security because threats were, and still are, moving faster than the explicit controls in each framework.

These frameworks offer an excellent foundation for security – but effective security programs must also remain responsive to new and emerging threats.

> • *Anyone using **only** a published framework to manage security is using something that is already 2 or more years behind what is required.*

Another challenge for many of the frameworks is that they often need to express objectives rather than explicit controls. In other words, they describe what should be achieved rather than how to achieve it. If they specify something, for example, a specific encryption standard, that choice can become outdated over time. But the speed of change forces frameworks to work in this way, by stating objectives rather than by describing explicit technical specifications.

For these reasons, it is great to use a framework to set the ground rules – but it is equally important to stay informed about new risks; this ensures that the overall strategy used to achieve effective security is kept agile and up to date with the threat landscape.

Trust-Based Security Fails

Auditors and attackers find it easy to identify a network's vulnerabilities. As soon as any security system relies on trust rather than on enforced processes, this makes it easy for attackers to find a way in.

> • *One in 10 people click on phishing links. One in 3000 people click on every single link and open every document they receive. Do not expect those numbers to change; fix the safeguards instead.*

As an example, phishing attacks work because people cannot do a better job of enhancing security than the security embedded in their devices does. If I wanted to construct a phishing attack that worked – I would only need to make the link or attachment in my email sufficiently interesting to the recipient.

User education can help to mitigate threats – but it will never fully eliminate the risks.

Anytime you rely on trusting people to do the right thing, rather than having controls to consistently detect and block risky activity, you have a trust-based vulnerability.

> • *Trust-based systems make easy targets for cyber criminals. Proactive security control-based systems deliver the most effective defense.*

Trust-based vulnerabilities have to be kept isolated (away) from systems and devices with information of value.

'Trust' issues most frequently arise with supplier systems, cloud services and mobile devices. If you do not have processes to consistently detect and block unsafe activities, expect that these deficiencies will be used as a way in.

Organizations with effective security never rely on trust to safeguard assets that are important to them.

Bribery

Another issue related to trust is the sticky subject of bribery. Fortunately, there are now strong anti-bribery and anti-corruption regulations. Unfortunately, not all organizations police these offenses.

It starts with items like champagne, flowers and free event tickets to luxury hotels for meals and drinks – items which exceed the limits most businesses place on gifts their employees may accept. If these items are acceptable without being declared, it ends up with six or seven figure contracts with direct or indirect kickbacks – including job offers for those people, their friends or relatives.

That decision to purchase certain services or products may not be based on the real value to the organization receiving it.

With already high and significantly increasing security budgets, there is very little not on offer to decision makers. What your organization buys can be strongly biased by bribery if gratuities and finances are not policed.

In an online anonymous survey I performed on security professionals, the majority of respondents stated that they had seen their management accept and be influenced by these types of gratuities.

Security events are exceptionally useful – and I am not averse to acceptable limits of corporate hospitality. However, I would similarly expect to openly declare any gratuities or financial interest BEFORE offering any advice or input into a decision. Vendors will naturally try to influence purchase decision makers, so it is essential any incentives received by employees are openly reported.

Fortunately, there are a larger number of environments where I have seen that bribery is not acceptable. The behavior seems to surface when hospitality is not monitored and failures to register interests are not subject to appropriate disciplinary measures.

Who Sells Outdated Security?

The rate of change means that security technologies are now in a constant state of flux and that the effectiveness of existing technologies degrades over time.

In addition, new technologies often start off being sold expensively as independent items, and shortly thereafter, the new technologies that work effectively end up being merged into more unified security packages.

An example of this can be seen in how web browser security operates.

For many years, just installing an anti-malware solution on a device could over-come most threats. If you surfed to a bad page that contained malicious software, your anti-malware solution could defeat it.

As that became decreasingly effective, a number of different solutions, with varying degrees of effectiveness, were increasingly adopted and initially sold separately:

- You could buy software that would pre-screen requests to visit any particular web address, and depending on the rule settings, either warn against or block access to that Internet location.
- You could run web sessions in 'containers' that could not spread any malware back onto the device, or even use virtual devices to help keep any malware away from the information or systems of value.
- New anti-malware built completely differently from traditional anti-malware became available that can block over 99% of threats.

The challenge this creates is three-fold:

(i)   It takes time for new vendors' products to become widely known and distributed.
(ii)   None of these security measures are 100% effective.
(iii)   It is often unclear which combination or which particular items to choose.

Most of us rely on listening to the most publicized and available information about what to do. This information tends to favor what has been most effec-tive and not what is currently the best solution.

One of the most striking things about going to security events is that the secu-rity technologies with the largest stands and most accessible distribution are often the worst ones to buy.

It is important to keep this in mind. It is usually a very bad idea to enter into a multi-year deal for a security technology – because it is risky to assume that the technology is and will continue to be effective.

Be careful to evaluate any security technology carefully. Is it really the most effective approach? How long is it expected to be useful for?

Traditional anti-virus solution approaches may be dead, but look for newer security technology with >99% effectiveness and you will see it is out there. Yet your preferred supplier may not be stocking what you need – they may just be selling what they have.

The problem with suppliers trying to sell organizations outdated products because that is what these suppliers have and are accustomed to installing affects businesses large and small. In fact, a conversation between a small business customer and a technology service provider could effectively be translated like this:

Service Company: We would like to connect your systems together in a way that no longer makes sense but does mean that any successful attack will most likely spread like wildfire and any attacker will be able to easily hold your company to ransom.

Customer: Hold on, what is the chance this 'network' used by a few tens of people will get one of these malicious software attacks?

Service Company: Close to 100%

Customer: So why are you selling this?

Service Company: It used to work and we are trained to install it PLUS people are still buying it.

Customer: Is there no way to defeat these threats?

Service Company: Not that we sell or know about.

This scenario arises more and more often because the usefulness of networks to all types of businesses is rapidly diminishing. For many years, networks were very useful, since they interconnected devices to more easily share information.

With the progression of the Internet and mobile computing, networks are only useful in certain circumstances at the present time. If you have a manufacturing plant or closed network you want to protect, they can still be managed securely with the right controls in place and by isolating and controlling what connects and happens in them.

But for most organizations, networks are now more dangerous than they are useful. If you have tens, hundreds or even thousands of individually secure devices that don't interconnect or trust each other – it is much harder to be subject to a cyber attack.

Problems like the one illustrated above in the supplier-small business customer conversation have resulted from the fact that the companies that service these businesses have not kept pace because they still often believe that networking devices together is a really good idea.

Fortunately, this situation is changing rapidly. The more that network attacks are successful, the more these service companies and their customers are waking up to keeping their systems secure in as many layers as possible – collaborating through layered defenses, sustaining regular backups, establishing easy restoration processes and implementing newer, more effective security solutions that outpace those that are no longer effective.

If you don't want to be implementing ineffective security, care has to be taken to evaluate whether purchases and decisions are part of an effective security strategy. Otherwise you too could be looking to buy or rent something that is yesterday's security.

6: Security by Design

You may have noticed that this book intentionally avoids pushing out explicit technical advice.

Putting effective cybersecurity in place cannot be achieved by explicit technical measures alone. Full, effective and responsive coverage is dependent on having a full range of processes that embed security from the very beginning into each and every technology and information service an organization uses and is reliant upon.

These security processes also need to include sufficient agility so security specialists can continue to rely on them to detect, respond and upgrade countermeasures as cyber threats evolve.

One day, a control is effective, but the next day it may not be.

A great example is the USB hacking key. Take any laptop, desktop or server where you have physical access and the belief was that if no user was actively logged in, it could not be accessed. Then a 'special' USB key was released. Simply plug it in and 13 seconds later – ta da – you are logged in with access to the device's resources. Details about the USB key became publically available in September 2016, although earlier versions of the same device are alleged to have existed for many years.

The key worked on the understanding that even when a device was locked, the USB port protocol would still run and install any USB device connected to it.

Of course, the operating system providers worked quickly to do what they could to defeat this tool.

However, this is a great example of the need for 3 things:

- You need layers of security – not just dependence on one thing.
- You need to adapt and respond quickly to new threats.
- You need processes to embed these capabilities consistently across your information and technology of value.

Of those 3 items, the last one (processes) is the enabler for the other two.

If you are on a boat that has many holes in the hull and is taking on water, what do you do first?

- Bail the incoming water out?
- Fix the hull?

Although you may need to bail out water to keep the ship afloat during the hull repair, until you address the gaps in the hull, the water will continue to flood in. Fixing the hull – in the context of security, is about having processes that ensure you consistently have security by design.

Cyber criminals go after the low-hanging fruit – the easy targets. Organizations that have comprehensive security by design are passed over by criminals because they are hard targets.

Implementing comprehensive security by design is nowhere near as difficult or expensive as it initially sounds. Conversely, trying to add security after the fact is monumentally difficult and expensive.

Embedding security by design delivers security at a cost that is thousands of times cheaper and tens of times faster than fixing something that is already broken.

> - *Fix the causes of security gaps before fixing the symptoms. There is no point in bailing water out of a boat riddled with holes. Fix key security processes and other root causes first, and then you can address the symptoms permanently without fear of them continually returning.*

Consider this example:

Imagine that you have a typical mix of applications that support your business which require low, medium, or high levels of security. As a new CISO, you might discover that they are randomly deployed to optimize cost on whatever infrastructure was available. If you want to implement layers of additional security on your highest-value items, it is not possible to do so without disentangling this mess.

Fixing the hull means implementing processes to ensure that all new deployments of technology are routed to areas specifically designated for applications that require low, medium or high levels of security.

Bailing the water means transitioning the existing systems onto environments designed to support their security needs.

If you bail the water first, then new technologies will continue to add to your problems as you address the already-present problems.

Cost Efficiency of Security by Design

Putting the correct security into a new technology is thousands of times – and I mean thousands of times – cheaper than trying to repair the problem after the technology is in large-scale use.

Security is not up to the developers (the people who program what you need) – they only do what they are paid and told to do.

Security is only as good as the processes that demand it. Security has to be embedded into the requirements for all working practices that create, install, operate and decommission technologies.

If you think of the typical lifecycle of a technology, it roughly goes like this:

- Someone identifies a business need.
- The technology to realize the business need is identified
- It is built and deployed
- The business (and maybe the customers) use it

If I put the right security requirements in place when the technology is being evaluated, it might result in a change of decision or the inclusion of certain specifications. The associated costs may be just hundreds or low thousands of dollars.

If I miss that step, I might discover the issue partway through the development or configuration. At that point, I did the equivalent of driving a car off the sales lot and then discovering I needed to retrofit something. At that point, the mitigation costs are substantially higher (tens or hundreds of thousands of dollars).

If the technology gets fully released and used widely, and then I discover some major security gaps, the cost and complexity has now reached eye-watering levels. Major organizations may be looking at costs in the hundreds of thousands to millions of dollars – without even considering the indirect costs from any business interruptions that retrofitting the technology may cause.

A piece of malware called 'Mirai' was a great example of the consequences of not incorporating security by design. After the October 2016 DDoS facilitated by Mirai, researchers discovered that millions of Internet of Things smart devices, such as Internet-connected CCTV recorders, had been shipped with hard-coded (unchangeable) usernames and passwords. Any basic security requirement that had been embedded into the development process would have prevented the vulnerability.

Problem: inadequate security assessment and requirements during the build.

Symptom: items were shipped with hard-coded usernames and passwords.

Low cost solution: include adequate security requirements and assessments from the early design stage.

High cost solution: fix the problem retroactively (after discovery).

The brands that had released the vulnerable devices and wanted to continue to sell them had to absorb tens of millions of dollars in costs to recall and fix their devices. They were forced to go for the high-cost solution. Considering the security requirement up front would have cost, at most, a few thousand dollars.

- *Security is thousands of times cheaper when embedded by design from the earliest stage. Security is not a paint that can be applied at the end. Applying security later on is more expensive than starting over is.*

Proactive vs. Reactive Security

Security by design is about understanding how to implement proactive security as well as incorporating processes that ensure reactive measures are taken promptly in response to new threats and risks.

Recent cybersecurity frameworks tend to break the steps into these five or more stages:

- **Identify**   (your valuable assets)
- **Protect**   (with appropriate security)
- **Detect**   (any compromised account or device)
- **Recover**   (replace or restore any compromised asset)
- **Respond**   (correct or update security)

Security by Design		
Proactive	\/ Identify	Defense by Design
	\/ Protect	
Reactive	\/ Detect	Protection from Detection
	\/ Recover	
	\/ Respond	

The first two steps (identify and protect) encompass the opportunities to implement *proactive* security by design. From here on in, we will refer to this as **'Defense by Design'**.

The last 3 steps are about monitoring and maintaining vigilance and responding to security issues *reactively*. We will refer to this as **'Protection from Detection'**.

During the proactive steps, every technology and service of value that can be identified, will be. Security will be considered and implemented from the earliest opportunity.

The reactive steps offer a more expensive, but still vital, opportunity to rapidly upgrade security as new threats materialize.

Each step in this sequence is equally important. Missing or performing any step ineffectively will result in substantial security vulnerabilities. However, it is the initial steps that offer the opportunity to cost-effectively put appropriate security in place. Waiting until the reactive steps come into play is much more expensive.

Remember the rule from earlier:

> • *The extent to which your last lines of cyber defense get triggered and used (for example - recovery management and information loss prevention alerts) is an effective measure of how many gaps you have in your primary security defenses.*

It is easy to tell when a security function is running well. The activities supporting the reactive steps are only firefighting if (i) they discover part of the business has failed to follow the defense by design processes or (ii) after a major new zero-day threat is discovered.

The Security Layers

In this chapter, we will only cover the very basics of the security by design approach. If you want more details – go to the second edition of *Cybersecurity for Beginners*.

The most fundamental layer is to get the **governance** correct.

Governance sets out the full set of policies and procedures that will ensure your organization has security by design embedded into every security operation.

This governance has to cover all of the technologies and electronic information of value for which an organization is responsible. These technologies and information assets are identified by having a consistent business process to capture a full and authoritative list of information assets. This process is known to security professionals as the **data governance** process.

> • *Your information of value, and where you allow it to travel, defines where you need your security.*

Electronic information of value flows around to service organizations just like water flows around a plumbing system. By capturing the information assets, and having proactive processes, it is then possible to put effective security into any pipe (application, device, communication route or other digital service) where you plan to allow it to flow.

This information allows security professionals to discover which technologies their security processes need to target for the installation of appropriate embedded security.

Once this proactive approach is in place, if you plan to add a new information asset, it gets logged into the asset register. If you plan to create a new application to support it, the business now has proactive processes to ensure appropriate security can be included by design from the outset. This will ensure that the following steps are taken:

- Security is included from the start of the requirements stage.
- Security is checked and verified before a technology is released.
- Security is monitored and checked periodically throughout the lifetime of the information asset.
- Security is upgraded whenever new threats are uncovered.

The governance layer, together with an informed understanding of the information and technology in use, allows the security architecture to evolve when changing needs require it. Items like identity and access requirements can be included from the start.

Procuring a new technology? Again, the capture of the intended information asset will ensure that the security architecture will be able to specify the security requirements during the procurement process rather than trying to fix it later on.

In a simple model, the initial layers can be considered as:

- **Governance** – sets out the policies and procedures, including the need to consistently capture information assets, through data governance.
- The **information asset register** identifies where the data will flow and specifies what needs to be protected by appropriate standards. Those standards are also elaborated into an evolving security architecture.
- The **security architecture** – elaborates the policies and procedures into actionable requirements on all the technologies, right from the initial build or during the procurement of external technologies.

Together, these layers ensure that processes will then evolve to include all applications, servers, user devices, communication routes, supplier systems and other external services (such as cloud).

The information layer identifies exactly what needs to be subject to risk assessment and inclusion of security requirements.

Periodic reviews, enforced by process, re-check the security on a defined timetable.

Threat intelligence, security incident and event management and other reactive measures (such as enterprise risk analysis) help to ensure that anything that happens between checks is then identified and dealt with.

Large organizations and even nation states that operate these layers effectively do not suffer megabreaches.

If you think this sounds like a substantial task, it is not IF you remember this:

> * *The security function exists to provide processes, technologies and advice that enable the business to operate within their preferred risk tolerance level. Security personnel should not make direct business decisions.*

The security function does not have to have the manpower to collect all of the information asset register. They only need to set up the process and educate those who will be responsible for doing this to ensure it is captured. The follow-on processes can similarly be substantially automated.

There are even some governance, risk and compliance security solutions that allow you to get almost all of these interlinked processes straight out of the box as a starting point.

The most frequent failure point is failing to even know what information needs to be protected in the first place.

> * *Your largest vulnerabilities often result from failing to put essential security processes in place. Your next-largest vulnerabilities result from failing to address the critical and major gaps that the processes identify.*

New Technology is Highest-Risk

The technology most open to late-stage realization that security is missing is the new stuff.

A typical process deficit example can be found in organizations that use supplier or cloud technology. Instead of understanding the security requirements before the service is even procured, when the realization happens later on, the cost is much, much higher. This is especially true if the chosen provider simply does not offer the security controls you require.

Processes have to cover everything of value – but the items that are newest are the ones that most frequently lead to the largest megabreach potential.

Whenever a new technology is being considered – the very first thing to do is to actively think about the security.

Over the next few years, mixed reality holographic computing and progression of the Internet of Things are two emerging technologies that require early consideration of security requirements.

Although my own holographic computer (a Hololens) is running on an established operating system (Windows 10) – I still had to think through certain security considerations. Should my employees be permitted to drive wearing it? How much more likely is an employee to allow a family member or friend to use it, even if that is against the rules? What new security issues might lending it out cause? Is it safe for a child to use?

Mixed and augmented reality will become regulated in a few years. However, there are substantial advantages to identifying and addressing the security issues early on. This is covered further in the chapter on how cybercrime is anticipated to evolve.

Security by Design in Practice

From the examples in this book and the vast number of organizations experiencing megabreaches, you may be under the misleading impression that security by design is difficult to implement.

Naturally, this book has provided examples of situations in which security by design is not in place to illustrate the probable consequences.

But when security by design is used in the real world, it works very well and I have helped to implement it in several organizations. When it is implemented, it transitions in very smoothly and provides massive benefits. Security becomes an enabler and a business advantage.

The main obstacles to implementing proactive security in any organization are the human factors, since it does require endorsement from both the executive and overall security manager – and it also requires substantial changes to how security operates.

However, once it starts to roll out, it is swiftly embraced.

Imagine that you are the CISO of a large organization that has just suffered a major cybersecurity breach. A copy of a significant number of personal records has been stolen.

'You can never fully secure information,' is the go-to line most often used to justify the breach.

In our hypothetical example, let's consider that the data contained at least some information from European Union (EU) citizens and that the new EU General Data Privacy Regulation is in force. This regulation carries a fine of up to 4% of a company's revenue, if investigators determine any negligence in the company's management of that type of data.

So what are the chances the company would be able to pass all of the following checks:

- Did they have an accurate register of the information?
- Was the system or systems that were compromised subject to regular reviews to ensure that adequate security was in place?
- Had any major or critical gaps been addressed?

An organization running security by design will be able to answer yes to all three of these questions. It will also be able to file a claim on any reasonable cyber insurance policy.

Best of all, the likelihood that such a breach will even happen to this organization is extremely low. After all, no megabreach happens without at least three critical or major gaps being present to be leveraged.

It is true that if you are operating systems containing security by design over public channels like the Internet, there will continue to be some minor compromises. However, with the right security embedded by design, those compromises will never be of megabreach proportions.

Although it is essential for organizations to detect and recover from those minor compromises, the vast majority of the intrusions that are discovered are preventable.

> • *It is the gaps that get targeted, not the working defenses. Don't allow the security you do have to reassure you; find out what you don't have.*

In summary, security by design enables an organization to gain holistic coverage of its digital ecosystem, including the pieces that exist outside its corporate network.

Security by design also provides security at a much lower cost.

> • *Security measures must deliver tangible benefits and value that exceed both their direct and indirect costs, or they will not be implemented.*

Lean and efficient processes soon prove their worth. Smaller costs are transferred into the implementation of new technologies and services, and larger, reactive costs are substantially reduced.

One of the best features in this approach is this:

If you implement the right processes, you no longer have to reactively identify and resolve legacy (existing) security issues. Those pre-existing issues will identify themselves through the processes and allow the business units to actively identify the problems, leaving the security function to consult and move the security position to a better place.

7: Cybersecurity and Cybercrime Evolution

Megabreaches do not come about because the right security is not available. They occur because the right security is not implemented.

Getting caught out by cyber attacks used to be rare. Then the incidence of cyber attacks exploded. First these attacks targeted large organizations, and then they quickly began affecting huge numbers of private individuals and small businesses.

The rate of cybercrime and the enormous amount of money it makes will continue to grow for a few more years.

Security is beginning to catch up, but with low cybersecurity standards having spawned such a large, lucrative worldwide cybercrime industry, what is set to change over the coming years? When will cybercrime fall back to less pandemic levels? What will cybercrime look like in the future?

The main progressions to expect that are explored in this chapter are:

1) The situation is set to get worse before it improves. Internet outages will happen. Megabreaches will continue for awhile yet.
2) Cybersecurity will improve and get simpler for humans to rely on – but that will increase the focus of cybercrime onto scams and psychological manipulations (confidence tricks) targeting individuals. Individuals who have legitimate access to cyber systems will constitute the easiest attack point and the most convenient route around technical security measures.
3) Scams and psychological manipulations directed at individuals will become more persuasive than ever. Personal information combined with something called **machine learning** will make it more difficult for people to resist falling for cyber criminals' schemes and will make the resulting personal losses more devastating.

Megabreaches and Digital Disruptions Continue

It turns out that humans find it difficult to keep up with the evolution of technology. We constantly innovate and create new things, without including the right security measures from the outset.

The Internet itself turns out to be based on inadequate and unsecure principles that need to be updated. All of the different layers involved in Internet communications and operations were never designed with the volume, usage and speed for which they are now being used. This means that many of the layers have gradually become susceptible to new types of subversive usage. Even the most harmless of Internet communication protocols, such as sending website links, can now be used to help send stolen information slowly out of an otherwise secure environment. This technique is rather like the tactic in the film *The Great Escape*; instead of sand hidden in trouser legs, the criminals hide large volumes of small amounts of stolen information as fictitious website requests.

Motivated by the large financial incentives that drive cybercrime, every layer of Internet operations is being investigated and used for nefarious opportunities. This momentum is further driven by the continuous expansion in the bandwidth of Internet connections and the proliferation of low-cost Internet-connectable devices.

Put simply; there have been more and more cyber opportunities emerging that are getting easier and easier for the criminals to take advantage of.

Many of my friends and colleagues mistakenly think I am either a master hacker or run a crime ring. They get concerned that I have insider knowledge about threats.

What really happens is that I will mention something to them – such as 'Do you trust your banks?' and will talk about the security issues, and then, under a week later, something really big will hit the news relating exactly to that topic.

One example of this happened recently. I sat opposite a friend in a coffee shop. I had not seen him for about 6 months. The topics of conversation were wide ranging – but we had both been working on the same security program. Inevitably, the topic of security came up.

I mentioned a new DDoS technique leveraging the Internet of Things that was about to take down sections of the Internet. Two days later Twitter and several other major online services were taken down by exactly this technique.

When I started writing this book, Internet brownouts were not happening in developed countries. But right after I predicted the huge DDoS attack, it did happen.

The challenge with predicting the future is that it is now happening so fast that you are likely reading this and thinking 'well that already happened' – so look at the edition date and note that it was predicted.

Do I have clairvoyant powers? Or do I actually run a crime ring and use the techniques that are causing these events I predict, as my friends have suggested? In truth, I anticipate these megabreaches because I stay updated on current threats, hacking techniques, and security solutions. So right now I can say that in terms of digital disruptions, there will be a short-lived time when access to the Internet will be taken down for days at a time. There will be attacks that take out critical parts of the Internet service layer, effectively browning out entire countries or sections of countries.

It turns out that the Internet itself did not have security by design. Nobody predicted that there would be armies of millions of infected devices connected to the Internet. Nobody foresaw that a technique like the one that caused the recent DDoS attack could be directed to focus unmanageable volumes of data requests anywhere on the Internet, taking down online services.

The Internet will adapt, and will eventually be able to deny and disable these attacks – but those attacks will happen for a time before the architecture and design of the Internet infrastructure is improved to defeat them.

As I write this book, you can connect anything to the Internet, no matter how unsecure or infected it is.

What will change is that Internet connections will soon be denied to devices that prove themselves to be untrustworthy. This will essentially be an Internet dress code. If your device is not wearing the right kind of security, it will be denied access.

There will also be far more Internet connection channels available, making it far harder for any would-be attacker to disconnect services or connections. Instead of relying only on local connections, devices will be able to choose from a range of local and global connections to get to the Internet.

As an example, Elon Musk (founder of Tesla and SpaceX) is planning a global array of satellites with hyper connectivity capabilities. Unless the North Korean government can blow those satellites out of the sky, their people will be able to tap into rich new networks of connectivity, potentially free of any control or censorship.

Within a few years, Internet connectivity, even for private individuals, will not be state controllable. There will be so many choices for connecting to the Internet that cyber attacks will no longer be able to disrupt Internet connections. In fact, only a military-grade electromagnetic pulse (**EMP**) would be able to disconnect a country.

This means that nation states will not be able to block an Internet-based service by simply exercising control over the Internet infrastructure that lies within their jurisdiction.

Like attacks that disrupt Internet service, megabreaches will also continue to occur for a few more years.

This is because the majority of organizations still have large numbers of security gaps in their core technologies. As we have already covered, it is not that these gaps are unfixable – simply that the human motivations and decision factors are stacked against ensuring that these flaws are fixed before substantial breach and disruption events occur.

Banks have long been a key target of cyber criminals. After all, they have the immediate money in which these criminals are most interested. Bank security is not great, and most banks are managing cyber attacks by refunding customers, paying ransoms or not disclosing attack information for fear that their customers will lose confidence in the bank's ability to hold onto their funds.

In turn, cyber criminals are allowing banks to operate – because it suits them to slowly scrape, steal and ransom them. As security improves, I anticipate something as large as the Yahoo breach that impacted hundreds of millions of customers will emerge in one or more major banks. It will turn out that some cybercrime gangs have long had full access to core financial systems at some of the largest banks.

At the point when security is about to turn a corner, it will no longer suit the cyber criminals to slowly pick away at those financial institutions.

Cyber heists currently aim to only steal millions of dollars from each bank at any one time – because the criminals know they can mostly get away with it.

The only reason that billions are not taken is that the potential impact of a heist of that magnitude could be to kill off your benefactor. To steal a large amount of money successfully requires that the impact is shared. Market and exchange rate manipulations with profits in the hundreds of millions of dollars have taken place. However, the banks and financial institutions did not pay; instead, the investors covering the opposite trade position did.

But once the major banks come close to implementing upgraded, effective security, cyber criminals will stop worrying about the true impact of a multi-billion dollar breach, and one or more of these major banks will turn out to be open to a megabreach that they cannot afford to cover. When that happens, it could lead to the collapse of any or all of these banks.

This has already been seen on a smaller scale in smaller banks, such as the breach in November 2016 that affected Tesco Bank in the UK. Once these banks' systems were successfully compromised, the banks immediately prevented their customers from accessing their own funds for a time while they took remedial actions.

Just like banks did during the bank runs of old and more recently during the financial crisis in Greece that started in 2010, withdrawals may have to be limited to protect these institutions.

State intervention will be necessary to protect customers from the consequences of these breaches. In some cases, states are already starting to intervene by regulating the security of technology.

At some point, any critical service, including banking, will not be allowed to operate under self-regulated security inspections. Banks and other institutions will be expected to pass state inspections that assess the suitability of their security measures.

> • *Criminals share information better and faster than legitimate organizations do.*

Another reason that cyber breaches will continue to occur, at least for the foreseeable future, is that, as noted, cybercrime networks are fast to share information about new vulnerabilities, while legitimate companies are slow to do the same.

A cybercriminal can share vulnerability information and get immediate support and advice from the entire criminal community on how to exploit it.

Most legitimate organizations dare not share information about their vulnerabilities until they have independently worked out how to fix them.

This situation will help to perpetuate the opportunities for cybercrime in the foreseeable future.

The lesson is simple. Organizations that can use technology securely will prosper and those that cannot will be marginalized or even completely disappear.

The cyber criminals will inadvertently help to weed out the vulnerable. Just like the evolutionary principle that species which evolve to meet changing environmental conditions are the ones that survive, the organizations that adapt to provide safe new technologies with great security by design will survive.

In line with this weeding-out process, expect to see further, massive megabreaches affecting the core technologies of some of the largest organizations on the planet.

Cybersecurity Improves

The security of technology is becoming too complicated to be operated by humans. The constant evolution of new technologies and new threats requires knowledge and understanding that outpace our capacity to cope.

I monitor and research how this progression is happening.

In the past, we have embraced security technologies that work for awhile – and then continued to embrace them after they stopped being the most effective option.

An example of how changes to security technologies are outpacing human decision-making processes can be seen in how anti-malware software installed on user devices is managed.

By late 2016, there was a consensus that traditional anti-malware software was not very effective. It was better than having nothing at all, but was no longer effective for detecting or blocking the majority of malicious software technologies used by different types of attackers.

The way that these (now outdated) solutions worked was to wait for a piece of software to run, and, based on its unique properties (its *signature*), to identify what it was and to then disable and often remove it.

Traditional anti-malware providers had teams of staff dedicated to decrypting and dissecting new threats, and to then creating updates to the software that would block them. As the volume of new threats increased from a few hundred per day to thousands and then hundreds of thousands, the model no longer provided the level of protection it once did.

The dominant anti-malware providers had a solution with only partial effectiveness and large numbers of staff trying to keep a defensible level of protection in place.

Meanwhile, customers often had multi-year contracts in place committing them to continue to use those partially-effective solutions.

Unburdened by these constraints, a small number of very clever and innovative new companies developed a more effective approach. These new solutions used new techniques called artificial intelligence and **machine learning** to identify threats, mostly before these threats even started to operate. One of those companies demonstrated their technology to me.

Machine learning *is the ability of a software program to educate itself to recognize new patterns and processes without the need for direct human intervention.*

Two hundred malware threats were downloaded to 2 different computers. One of those machines ran traditional anti-malware software and the other ran the company's new security technology.

They asked me to guess how many of the threats each type of security technology would identify and block. My guess was close. I knew that their software had an alleged 99.7% success rate and that the outdated anti-malware technology was only about 40% successful.

Their demo sample contained 100 'known' malware threats and 100 that had been modified in a way that many attackers typically use on malware, using readily available tools. (Modifying can adjust multiple features of any malware to make it look different from its earlier incarnation).

The traditional technology captured about 40% of the known threats. My guess was about right. I thought zero of the modified threats would be captured. In fact, I was wrong. Within a few minutes, the modified threats had started multiplying. Not only had the old technology not captured them, but worse, there were now twelve more new threats.

Conversely, the new security technology had identified and prevented all of the threats from becoming active, including those that had been modified, and it had not required any of them to be run before detecting and blocking them.

In fact, the US Office of Personnel Management installed this new tech after their 2015 breach. It immediately found and blocked over 2000 pieces of malware that the existing, traditional anti-malware had missed.

This is great news – the development of a new security technology that tramples all over threats to digital devices is a huge improvement. This technology is about to become more widely available, and it will help to reduce the number of attacks.

However, there are other new security technologies that are not quite as effective or reliable, and these innovations have varying degrees of success. There are so many of them, it can be difficult to determine which ones represent the best value for the money – and which are a complete waste of money.

In fact, there is a continuous stream of new security technologies emerging. Some of them are terrible and are very short-lived. Some are ingenious and provide substantial improvements.

The best new security technologies tend to be sold separately at first and then become integrated into easier-to-deploy mainstream products.

An example of this was a product based on the concept of isolating web browsers from the devices that were using them to access the Internet. This technique, a form of **containerization**, helps to prevent most URL/Internet-based threats from reaching devices. The browser window is effectively isolated away from being able to communicate or infect the device operating system.

This was initially sold only as a standalone product and was then integrated into some leading operating systems.

The step improvement in cybersecurity will be brought about by the seamless but nearly invisible inclusion of these new, intelligent security technologies that manage vast numbers of issues – with only minimal questions and notifications to the person operating the device.

This means the security on whatever computing devices we use will return to near-perfect levels within a few years.

In large organizations, however, it will still be important to ensure that security is embedded by design in electronic information and the information systems used to manage it.

At the present time, organizational security is left to individual management choices. Soon, there will be hyper-intelligent software that will be able to pull a far more structured analysis and control into place.

Security by design will cease to be difficult to figure out. Even if an organization forgets to implement the right security, there will be technologies that are able to rapidly and organically identify, analyze and resolve security issues.

Machine learning and artificial intelligence applied to organizational security will allow security functions to implement best practices more easily than has been possible in the past.

So what will that mean for cybercrime? What happens when security is strong and only legitimately authorized people can access systems?

It means that those legitimate users remain the easiest point to target and compromise.

Mostly, targeting legitimate users has meant stealing usernames and passwords. So will that still be what the cyber criminals are after in the future?

Increased Personal Attacks

One of the many challenges for cybersecurity is that access to systems is still mostly reliant on issuing passwords and usernames to people who need to access them.

Added to that, most private individuals are lousy at creating secure passwords and rarely use unique ones for each service they access.

This creates a big problem for organizations. Cyber criminals can steal one legitimate username and password and have a high likelihood of being able to re-use this information successfully on a completely different system a person uses.

Implementing supposedly failsafe security techniques such as requiring users to answer memorable questions, such as 'What is your mother's maiden name?' turned out to be a really bad practice. Most people use and answer questions that almost anyone can answer after performing an Internet search, and many also use the same questions on multiple platforms.

To make sure that only a particular individual gains access to his or her online services and information, passwords will soon be just a secondary form of confirming the person's identity.

Instead of passwords, most people will authenticate their access to systems by simply being who they are. Biometrics such as facial recognition technologies can already be used to access some operating systems.

More sophisticated biometrics will verify that the person accessing a system is the right person by verifying multiple aspects of who they are. For example, biometrics will check the individual's voice pattern as well as his or her face.

Geographic locations and individuals' activity patterns can also help to detect and block unauthorized access. If you are in one country one second and then try to log in from another country a few seconds later – one of those attempts is clearly not valid.

As identity and access authorization get a lot smarter, your computing devices will start checking multiple personal qualities before permitting you to initiate or authorize any transactions.

This will make people fully accountable for what happens in their online accounts. The responsibility for security and authenticating transactions will become undeniably linked to the owner of each account.

In terms of cybercrime, this makes cyber mugging and social engineering a much more attractive method of attack.

This already happens a lot. It will soon happen even more.

Lonely people are already targeted in this way, convinced to send money to some kindred spirit perhaps thousands of miles away who needs money to travel to see the victim, or to resolve some made-up personal dilemma.

Advances in artificial intelligence and machine learning mean that understanding and exploiting the psychology of potential individual victims is about to get much easier.

If I cannot steal access to individual accounts – the easiest way is to persuade or convince people to perform that transaction for me.

Scams are nothing new. What is new is just how easy it will be to profile and target people with interactions and offers that are far more compelling than they ever used to be.

For many years, low-level phishing scams have involved sending out fake emails, often with spelling and grammar mistakes. Did you know that those typographical errors are often intentional? After all, if you failed to notice those errors, the criminals know you are more likely to fall for the next part of their scam – and to ultimately be tricked into giving the criminals the information or access they are after.

However, it is easy to successfully compromise even the brightest of targets. All the criminal needs to do is to better understand his or her target. If the criminal can hide the attack as part of a usual task the person performs, the chances of success are close to 100%.

If I know where you like to shop, it might be that a high-value discount voucher is offered from what appears to be a genuine source. If you receive a PDF voucher or link from a service you subscribe to and regularly use, the likelihood that you would open the file or link is very high.

At the present time, it takes time and effort to profile a specific target and to gather information about his or her habits, hobbies and other interests. It takes even more time to then create an attack that you know will be compelling for the individual.

However, technologies are now able to automatically find much more information about targets than they used to be capable of achieving.

Have you seen the YouTube video called 'Mindreader'?

In it, a pretend mystic invites a random stranger into a tent where the people appear to have a fantastic level of knowledge about the random person. At the end of each segment, a curtain drops to reveal a team of people who used all the information available online to find out who the person is, who their friends are, what they bought recently and more.

With the evolution of technologies and machine learning, very soon you will not need a team of people to pull that information together in real time. I could sit in a train station, wearing an untethered holographic computer (Hololens is the first of these) and using new software (not yet available at the time of this writing) that can place little tags over the passers-by.

This holographic computer allows a view of the real world to be blended with views of digital information. I can look out through clear lenses and see both two and three-dimensional images and information projected into real space. The computer can see everything I can – and a lot more.

As people pass by, I can now find out who they are – and with a single air gesture, read all of the information that it used to take a team of people to find.

This is possible because these days, most of us want to interact online, and many of us choose to share enormous amounts of personal information. Whatever any of us does online leaves a trail of valuable information.

Added to that, existing laws in many countries allow officials to put far too much information about their citizens online as well.

I could sit outside the gate of a company and know more about each person who walked out than most of their colleagues do. Where they live, what they recently shopped for, what they like to look at online and more...

I could drive down a street and know how much each property cost, who lives there, perhaps how much they earn, what the interior of their property looked like the last time it was on the market...

If you read this in 2017 – you might think 'wow,' but if you read it after 2018, you will probably think, 'Meh.'

Not that this will be the primary way in which cybercrime evolves – but it certainly starts to open up new opportunities – and already has.

In late 2016, a hack that stole very basic information about some customers (name, address and what they just purchased) was used to target them to steal their new purchases.

Most people have far too much personal information openly available online. That information will get easier for anyone to pull together.

After all, as security improves, the one constant and easiest way to compromise security is to compromise the people who have legitimate access to whatever the criminals want.

The Future of Data Privacy

There is a question about whether our personal data will be more available or more protected in the future.

Regulations within some countries are aiming to give individuals greater control over their personal information.

Conversely, since many services rely on knowing more and more about their customers, there are an increasing number of global services that ignore, bypass or, at best, navigate these regulations.

Chances are good that the companies which do not comply with regulations will find it easier and easier to get away with it for several reasons. For one thing, countries will soon lose the ability to control Internet access, as discussed earlier in this chapter.

Data storage is also on a never-ending decline in price. This means that more people will be storing more personal data in various cloud platforms and other Internet locations.

These factors all contribute to the reality that since so many essential services rely on knowing a lot about us, it is unlikely that the amount of personal information available on the Internet will decrease.

Always expect that whatever you do online is tracked somewhere and might never be deleted. Take care about what you do online or what you choose to upload to reduce the chances that these activities will someday return to bite you.

As far as personal data goes, it is better to be a pessimist. A pessimist is never disappointed.

Countries will keep trying to regulate data and organizations will keep finding ways around these controls. After all, collecting personal information and fully understanding customers is the fastest route towards making a profit for these organizations.

Cyber Convergence and Cyber Physical Systems

There is a change coming. It is often referred to as Industry 4.0.

Industry 4.0 describes the blending of automation, machine learning (software teaching itself to do things better), faster communication speeds, more processing power and easier to access or build technologies to help deliver better goods and services more efficiently.

What industry 4.0 seeks to do is to leverage all of the transdisciplinary advantages into a combined, collaborative, automated and flexible arrangement.

This approach will affect all types of goods and services. The restaurant of the future might be fully automated, from its construction all the way through to the point at which a customer receives the food. The only organic components might be the food and the customers.

If any part in this supply chain breaks, the intelligent systems will be able to source and use alternatives without any visible disruptions.

Although industry 4.0 is in its infancy, the tremendous rate of technological change means that it will not be more than a few years until these systems are in regular and widespread use. Expect to see networks of autonomous vehicles running around and taking themselves off-road for servicing – and collaborating with other vehicles so they can all optimize what each component needs to do.

Cybersecurity is also starting to move in this direction.

We already began to look at how passwords will give way to more multi-dimensional forms of checking and verifying that each person who uses a device or performs an action is who they say they are. Criminals may be able to steal a single password or even potentially fake one personal attribute of a target – but once computers can verify your identity using multiple aspects of who you are – those opportunities for cyber attackers will disappear.

Whereas companies once needed people to understand and run complex layers of security, those same layers will soon be implemented by easier-to-use security technologies.

The new security technologies will use the same principles that underlie industry 4.0.

This will be advantageous for security, since, compared to computers, humans are slow to respond to threats and very inefficient when it comes to sharing information of value.

Many security functions and organizations to conceal information on threats and threat management as though they are competitive secrets. As platforms allow humans to learn faster and gives them access to more information about threats in real-time, the situation will change. As knowledge about threats and threat management become accessible faster and more universally, those organizations will no longer be on the back foot.

Cybersecurity machine learning is already happening. It powers the latest security products. It learns from a richer and wider pool of information than any human is capable of absorbing. It can update and block problems and threats in real time.

The emerging cybersecurity technologies provide a rich pool of defensive measures, based on something called ***cyber physical systems***.

These are self-learning, computer-based algorithms that can learn in a way that allows them to integrate new knowledge about authorized users and about program functions and resources. They can use their transdisciplinary capabilities to address problems in real time, and they can also figure out how to set up new network connections or how to shut off anything they determine to be rogue or harmful.

A cyber physical system is a tightly interwoven set of comprehensive perceptions that includes information about all the people, systems, technologies and other assets available. It can flexibly learn and adapt to sustain security, faster than any human can respond to these variables.

Cybersecurity is about to get a lot more powerful.

When these systems start improving security, some organizations – those that were already riddled with intrusions and threats they chose to ignore – will be brought down. This will happen because as these organizations upgrade their security, their attackers will panic when they realize that they are about to lose the cash cows they have been holding hostage. The attackers will then, in a desperate final bid to monetize these victims, put the victims' entire network contents up for sale.

However, even though these artificial intelligence and machine learning techniques will benefit some organizations, these same technologies will also give criminals new tools for committing cybercrimes. The technologies will make it easier for attackers to identify targets, and will also make it easier to manipulate those targets through the wealth of available personal information that allows the criminals to leverage social engineering techniques which they tailor to the victims' habits and preferences.

The transformation of security will also change the preferred targets for cyber criminals; instead of going after large organizations, they will increasingly target private individuals.

As security improves, the crimes of the future will also be more likely to affect people with authorized access to certain cyber networks, and will induce these victims to make transactions they regret, but cannot undo.

In the interim, before things improve, they will get slightly worse. We should all expect to see more disruptions to digital services and the failure of some very, very large institutions.

8: Blocking the Blockchain

Prevention of cybercrime is something in which we can all play a part.

Being aware of which behaviors contribute to and support cybercrime is part of the key to defeating it.

Most of the scams and attacks rely on all of us continuing to support the wrong behaviors. If more of us support the right behaviors, the financial motivation to commit cybercrime will very rapidly evaporate.

Never Pay Ransomware

Have you ever purchased stolen goods? Would you consider doing it?

Well, ransomware is effectively paying a criminal a fee to give you back something that is rightfully yours anyway. For this reason, paying ransomware is worse than buying stolen goods, since you are rewarding the very criminal who just stole something from you. It is actually doubly worse because each time a ransomware payment is made, the cybercrime industry grows and has funds to commit even more crime.

Each of us who directly or indirectly supports the payment of ransomware makes a contribution to the continuation of cybercrime.

If you find out that an organization you patronize is paying ransomware, switch to an alternative that does not.

If you have the misfortune of being subject to a ransomware demand, never pay up. Although it may seem cheaper and easier at the time, your action will result in the cyber criminals knowing that you are a valid target for more demands.

As Rudyard Kipling wrote in his poem *Dane-Geld*, 'Once you have paid him the Danegeld you never get rid of the Dane.' This refers to the fact that if you pay one ransom, the criminals know that, provided they compromise you enough, you will pay up. They will therefore continue to target you.

People who fall for scams and pay ransom demands are added to 'sucker lists.' These are lists of the people and organizations that are known to be susceptible to cybercrime.

The way that ransomware is designed to work is to make you believe that paying up has an upside that exceeds the costs. Remember to consider that the long-term impact of paying a ransomware demand is that you are responsible for adding your name to a sucker list and being subject to repeated ransom demands.

In November 2016, the San Francisco metro system was subject to a cyber attack on their ticketing system. They had a choice to pay a ransom or to let people ride the system for free while they fixed the problem. They wisely did not pay the ransom.

Paying the ransom may have seemed to be the more economical option. It would not have been. If they had paid up, they would have marked themselves as a much larger target for further attacks.

The evidence for this is clear. Those banks that have set-up their own Bitcoin accounts have done so to repeatedly pay up on the ransom demands, where others actually fix their security and pay nothing to the crime gangs.

We Need to Talk About Encryption

Encryption is often held up as a great enabler for security. It certainly is the foundation for some effective security technologies – but like any weapon, it can be used for both good and evil.

As already mentioned, cryptocurrency and, more specifically, the blockchain (the encryption-based technology that makes cryptocurrency possible) is the main enabler for cybercrime.

A wide range of financial service firms, government officials, and IT experts believe that blockchain is an incredibly useful technique that will lead to substantial changes in how everybody performs financial transactions.

The basic idea is that the blockchain offers a technique that allows transactions to happen directly between two parties without the need for a middleman. In cryptocurrency, that means that payment can be made between two parties with the technology being the only factor needed to complete the transaction.

The danger of using cryptocurrency, as has been demonstrated, is that the party making the payment has absolutely no recourse. The transactions that occur are anonymous and have no oversight or regulation. Effectively, blockchain makes international ransom drops and other types of illegal scams and money laundering transactions possible.

If cryptocurrency transactions were totally illegal, the entire cybercrime industry would almost totally collapse overnight.

> • *Cryptocurrency enables most cybercrime. If (or when) the blockchain gets defeated, the cybercrime industry will suffer a massive deflation.*

Fortunately, both encryption and the blockchain have several weaknesses.

> • *Encryption is a lock that degenerates over time. If you can sit and wait for long enough you can undo any form of encryption.*

If I had a copy of files that were protected by the best encryption available twenty years ago, they could be deciphered with the computing power of the average smartphone within a relatively short time.

Encryption is a technique that is only good for protecting information for a certain period of time. As computing power increases, the time it takes for the encryption to be decipherable decreases.

If (or when) the encryption behind Bitcoin is cracked, the cybercrime industry could be very close to being dismantled. Unfortunately that might take some time.

It is one of my main hopes that the blockchain will be defeated.

The same experts who believe that blockchain is the wave of the future also think that it is so robustly designed that it is undefeatable, or to be more precise, that the audit trail is impenetrable. However, I have spent a lot of time on supposedly undefeatable audit trails, and I can see some options for being able to take the currency down.

So – heed my request, and if you are inclined toward hacktivism that works in the best interests of humanity – find a way to bring it down. You would do more to stop cybercrime than anyone on the planet.

Here are some of the weaknesses:

With enough computing or botnet power, if more than 50% of the ledgers used to maintain Bitcoin are changed – the changed values become the accepted values.

If you insert invalid or unwanted transactions that are believed to be legitimate into the blockchain, those transactions cannot be expunged. They are locked in without any ability to reverse the documentation.

If the encryption is broken, then all Bitcoin balances become accessible and the currency will effectively collapse.

... and the great news is that as a globally unregulated and unaccountable currency, there would be absolutely no legal recourse for any of the people with Bitcoin balances.

Destroy confidence in Bitcoin and other cryptocurrencies and the economics of cybercrime would have to go back to the more challenging territory of trying to transact and launder legal currency.

When you stop to think about it, transactions made using encryption that happen across borders are effectively no different than allowing diplomatic baggage to pass through customs unchecked.

Although I do believe that privacy is desirable, I believe that security and crime are bigger problems. Our ecosystem might fare better with full transparency. If networks only permitted fully transparent communications, then everything would be open to scrutiny and that would give cybercrime no place to hide.

You might not like CCTV to be in place everywhere – but when you really think about it, these objections are based on the fact that it can capture everything that happens. The good and the bad.

Our technology transactions are really no different than images on camera. We should only fear making all of our activities public if that transparency is in some way an embarrassment or reveals activities that are illegal or unethical.

Although anonymity is desirable, few technologies are interested in providing it, and those that do usually have subversive intentions.

If unreadable content was blocked by default, it would enable a lot of cyber-crime to be defeated – but unfortunately, this is not a viable option. There are too many communication channels available, and many of those channels will soon be out of reach for any nation states that seek to block them.

In late 2016, Russia blocked the LinkedIn service from operating in their country, allegedly because Russian citizens' data was not held on Russian servers. They could do that because although the servers were not in their country, the connections for Russian citizens to access them *were* physically located in their country. As we know that will soon change.

When the UK government suggested an end to encryption in January 2015, there were many outcries. It was seen as both a gross invasion of privacy and also as potentially unachievable.

However, it is possible that some networks, including sections of the Internet, will opt into transparency. Yes – those information transactions may be intercepted – but those networks will operate without interruption. They will be able to detect and block intrusions.

Some organizations' networks do insist on working internally without encryption. Data is only encrypted (converted into unreadable characters) at the network perimeter and decoded by the recipient.

So what does the future hold for encryption?

Certainly, many transactions of information will continue to use encryption – but many of the most secure networks will be operating in ways that permit open inspection by removing or decrypting information for inspection before passing it on.

Stiffening the Penalties

If cryptocurrency transactions were totally illegal, the entire cybercrime industry would almost totally collapse overnight.

One of the biggest enablers of cybersecurity gaps and criminal activities is that many of the core activities that allow the problems to continue are without legal consequences.

Some banks openly trade this illicit currency. Should that really be acceptable?

Many legitimate organizations have also chosen to make certain transactions, including ransomware payments, in Bitcoins. Do you think that support for cybercrime should be legal?

A lot of effort is expended on looking at the symptoms, but very little action, legal or otherwise, is devoted to addressing the root causes.

Another example of a technology that supports crime without legal consequences is The Onion Router, or TOR, as it is more commonly known. This is a special piece of software designed to help people do things on the Internet without being detected.

You want drugs, guns, or to close down your rival? You want to view illegal images? All this and more is available on the dark and hidden underbelly of the Internet.

TOR works by masking and encrypting the standard identifiers that are used for network communications.

If I went out into the real world and engaged in any of these activities, I would quite rightly be arrested. Unfortunately, too many people seem to think that engaging in the same behaviors on the Darknet is acceptable.

One good disincentive for criminals would be if the regulatory penalties for being caught using the Darknet were severe. As I write this book, many of my colleagues and journalists spend unhealthy amounts of time exploring the Darknet in what they might refer to as research.

It makes no sense to a security practitioner that they can overtly engage and discuss how they explore the dark underbelly of the Internet quite legally.

We need to make proven use of the Darknet something illegal. The only people who should use it are criminals and law enforcement agencies.

It would be very easy for each and every country to put up significant penalties for accessing the Darknet and even harsher penalties for anyone found to intentionally host Darknet sites.

This would not be hard to do. Honeypot versions of TOR, where users think they are downloading the latest build but actually download something that reports all of their activities to their law enforcement unit is an example of the kind of process that would swiftly banish much of the Darknet use into the sewer where it belongs.

Legislation is being enacted to impose penalties on organizations that do not substantially improve their security position, but again, these half-hearted efforts represent an insufficient commitment on the part of governments to try to stop cybercrime. These regulations are not going to be too effective because the penalties amount to slaps on the wrist that will not really motivate these organizations to introduce significant changes. Most of the penalties are simply financial, when the approach that would really work would be to assign personal, criminal liability to substandard workmanship that results in harm or damage to others.

We do this for tangible crimes. If a health and safety problem results in someone's death, criminal charges will be brought.

> • *Do not expect organizations to stop doing something just because it is illegal. They only stop when the near-term fines and consequences outweigh the remediation costs.*

In the world of technology, in almost every country, it is possible for a company to set up and use technology so negligently that they can kill people – with little or no fear of any reprisals at all.

A great example of this can be seen with new augmented reality applications. They can use algorithms that are completely oblivious to the user's surroundings, and have already resulted in several deaths as people wandered onto private land or into minefields or other dangerous environments.

Even the more traditional technologies have the potential to result in death. Imagine if a piece of safety reporting software fails to work correctly. An alert that might have resulted in a warning that would save lives could be missed.

If you think these examples are minor, consider the changes that are happening. Could a flaw in the software that runs self-driving cars lead to large-scale failures that result in hundreds or thousands of simultaneous deaths?

What about the software running something like a nuclear power station? How much more care and attention might be taken if an accountable owner could face consequences if their work was subject to the same standards of regulation that are invoked for any other type of inappropriate health and safety decision?

Consequences need to drive peoples' decisions when the technologies for which they are responsible can directly result in death or harm to others. This does not happen at present.

So far, the number of deaths from shoddy cybersecurity has been low. They will not stay low without proportionate consequences.

Digital technologies have (so far) saved far more lives than they have cost. To keep it that way, we need stiff penalties for gross digital negligence; just like we already have stiff penalties for those who commit gross acts of physical negligence.

Stop Employing Criminals

Have you ever noticed how the poorly paid, heavily tattooed, multiply pierced security guard who turns up to cover the late shift looks like he or she is actually the type of person he or she is being paid to keep out?

In the world of cybersecurity, these are the grey hats.

White hats only use their hacking powers for good.

Black hats use them for unethical purposes.

Grey hats will do pretty much whatever they need to, in order to get money. Any black hat considering working for a legitimate company is, in fact, a grey hat.

It has become trendier to be a black or grey hat hacker than to be fully ethical. The majority of people under 25 think of these rogues as being more desirable and romantic than white hat hackers are.

Quite a number of legitimate companies are encouraged to rehabilitate these lovable rogues into security assets.

Although a fully reformed ex-criminal can be an asset, it has been my experience that hiring one or more people who really know how to hack, who have a past history of doing so with unethical intentions, requires a level of oversight that is seldom welcomed by the employee or available to the employer.

Yes – these people excel at swiftly identifying security gaps. The question is whether they will share information about the deficiencies – and if so, with whom?

Most of the grey hats I have met brag about how easily they can bring down their organizations' systems for days or weeks. In many cases, these statements are true, and these individuals could really do what they say they can do.

They swagger around companies as if they own them. They do this because they really do have the power to shut these companies down.

> • *Do not employ active criminals within a security department. Using self-confessed, unreformed cyber criminals (grey hats) to operate security introduces an extreme insider threat.*

The lesson here is to be sure that your 'asset' is truly an ex-criminal. If you employ people who continue to enjoy the darker side of hacking, expect the consequences.

The phrase used to be 'Beware of Greeks bearing gifts.'

The new phrase should be 'Beware of grey hats managing threat information.'

Nation states use a lot of grey hats. They don't expect these employees to do anything other than make criminal income outside of core hours – and to re-use the information they access. They only 'disconnect' these criminals if they find them doing something that conflicts with the nation state's goals.

If you want to harness the power of a grey hat, you have to know that the standard of security oversight will be stronger than the untrustworthy criminal. If not, you are entrusting the full security of your company to this individual, even if you did not mean to.

9: Do You Have a Megabreach Brewing

These days, being able to determine if any large organization you work for or deal with has rotten cybersecurity is a very valuable skill. After all, it helps to determine if the future of that organization is sustainable.

Making that determination is not very difficult at all.

One obvious indicator that the security is in a bad state is that many different usernames and passwords are required to access the systems inside a single organization. What that demonstrates is that the organization has inadequate security architecture. It lacks a central identity and access management system – and to any cyber attacker, that means that those identities will not be managed effectively.

When a company uses multiple log-in techniques, an attacker can be guaranteed that some of those systems will include accounts that should have been deleted or de-activated, or, better still, will probably also include some default administrative accounts that can be used to infiltrate and corrupt those systems.

As a hacker, if you want to cause a megabreach, some very simple questions that any employee (even those in the security function) will be happy to answer will let you know if your chances of achieving this goal are high.

Try it. Ask someone who works for a particular organization how many different log-ins they need to maintain. If you prefix the question with something like 'Wow. I am really struggling with the number of different usernames and passwords my organization expects me to remember,' you are likely to find out what you want to know. The next question you should ask is: 'How many do you have to manage at your place of work?'

Because so many people continue to literally lead hackers on a guided tour of their organization's security vulnerabilities, it may seem that cybersecurity departments should simply give up. In fact, if you were to believe some people, effective security is impossible. They believe we should open up the bank vaults because we can't keep the money safe. The nuclear reactors should be shut down because there is no choice but to leave them open to cyber attack.

However, people have been keeping these items and systems secure for decades. So, effective cybersecurity is possible too, even if an organization has really weak security, as evidenced by factors such as having multiple log-in requirements.

One reason these weaknesses persist is that most CEOs do not ask the hard questions of their cybersecurity departments:

- Is there a full list of the entire organization's information assets?
- Is there a security architecture that spans supplier systems, cloud services and social media platforms?
- Is there a single, well-managed identity and access system covering all of the organization's resources, not just employees, but also suppliers, contractors and customers who access company data?
- Are there security processes to rapidly evaluate and include new technologies requested by the business?

Another key performance indicator that is frequently missed is this:

> - *The extent to which your last lines of cyber defense get triggered and used (for example - recovery management and information loss prevention alerts) is an effective measure of how many gaps you have in your primary security defenses.*

The items that are triggering security alerts and recovery actions are symptoms of deeper security gaps. Items that trigger alerts or breaches inform both security management and the executive alike about what needs to be prioritized for repair. Investigating the root cause of any security alerts or incidents will quickly identify what has been missed.

Security incidents and events and security complaints from internal sources, customers and external security experts are the items that help to expose what the cybersecurity gaps are.

If you are using a service or are part of an organization where minor breaches and disruptions to service are a way of life, this is an accurate indication of the fragile and breakable cybersecurity that is in place.

Many security experts argue that perfect security is impossible. Although there is some truth to that statement, it is very possible to create security that is robust. It is possible to reduce security risks to fractions of a percent and to have failsafes to help reduce that residual risk even further.

The idea that information and technology assets cannot be managed securely is of course a distortion. It is a convenient half-truth that can be used to navigate around difficult situations without having to address the root causes.

Determining whether an organization has the potential for a megabreach is simply a matter of understanding whether it is missing security by design.

If an attacker can determine that an organization has a disjointed and incomplete approach to security, he or she will know that there are opportunities to take advantage of – and that intrusions, disruptions and thefts will all be possible.

Missing the Information Asset Inventory

Upon joining one organization, I asked this question: 'Do you have a single, authoritative information asset register?'

'Yes,' was the reply. Then there was a pause... 'Except it isn't the only one.' Then another pause... 'and it isn't very accurate and it is not maintained.'

It also turned out that the information asset register had all kinds of other gaps. It recorded no information at all about any cloud services, critical supplier systems, externally hosted websites or social media groups that they managed.

So this single, authoritative source turned out to be none of those 3 things. It was not authoritative, it was not the only one and it didn't contain anything close to accurate and complete information (not really a great source).

This situation is not rare.

The usual reason given for not having a complete information asset register (inventory) is that pulling together this information would be an impossible task.

I might also believe that was true if I had not achieved that goal for and with many organizations. As outlined in the chapter on 'Security by Design,' it is not the security department that needs to populate that inventory. All the security department needs to do is to ensure that there is a mandated and accessible process so the business itself can provide this information.

Running security effectively relies on understanding what needs to be protected. Without an accurate inventory of, at the very least, all of the critical, major and regulated information assets an organization is responsible for, there is no foundation that can be used to build effective security. It is also not possible to understand the full set of technologies upon which the information relies.

You may recall that megabreaches can only be brought about when there are three or more critical or major security gaps.

If there is no single, accurate, information asset register, it can be guaranteed that megabreach opportunities exist.

Think like A Cyber Criminal

Security functions have a propensity to focus on what they understand.

All a cyber attacker has to do is find out what the security function is not paying attention to.

> • *A skilled attacker knows your security weaknesses better than anyone in your company does.*

For an attacker to find a route to a megabreach, he or she only needs to look in the places that a typical security function may be ignoring.

It is reasonable for an attacker to assume that most security functions are overstretched. When that function is overstretched, it will have gaps just like the physical door example from Chapter One. The security function will be focused on closing up gaps that they can close. That same security function is likely to completely miss providing any security in the areas for which they have no processes or known expertise.

A skilled attacker will not be mounting an assault on the security you *DO* have in place, they are looking for what is missing.

The skilled attacker can make fast work of identifying those process gaps.

Relaxed supplier security, poorly-configured cloud services, outdated customer web portals, poor management of information assets, inappropriate record management and/or disgruntled staff – these are all easily-identified factors that an attacker will focus on when planning a megabreach.

It is unfortunate, but true, that large organizations rarely have an accurate understanding of who works for them. When you think beyond the direct employees to the contractors, the suppliers, the suppliers to those suppliers and the numerous devices and online services that exist outside the company networks, it is that footprint that often presents the most viable attack opportunities.

Effective security functions learn to think like their adversaries – they learn to pay attention to things like the security status of their outside suppliers.

If you learn to think like an attacker, you may be surprised at how easy it can be to identify the gaps.

In contrast, if you know that valuable information is entrusted to external services and individuals without effective, active and appropriate security, once again, it can be guaranteed that megabreach opportunities exist.

Security Ignoring What They Don't Understand

A brilliantly easy way for a cyber attacker to identify ripe opportunities is to specialize in compromising new technologies that organizations are adopting without being aware of the security issues.

This issue is frequently referred to as **Shadow IT** and also by the more marketing-friendly term of **employee led cloud adoption.**

Shadow IT is a term used to describe independent decisions to create or adopt technology – decisions made away from the officially sanctioned technology and security processes.

Employee led cloud adoption is a form of shadow IT in which online services are used for business purposes without going through any security checks or conforming to configuration requirements from the security function.

These problems occur more frequently in situations where the security function intentionally tries to avoid using and managing new technology at the pace required by their business units.

An effective security department will treat a new technology as an opportunity to learn, confirm and implement measures to sustain the protection of the information entrusted to it. However, most of us have seen that when it comes to new technologies, many security departments push back.

That means if you internally ask an organization to implement a new technology, you will sense that the security department – and perhaps even the technology department – does not want, or have the capacity, to provide a service for it.

In the worst case scenario, they may authorize a business unit to proceed alone, or with just some standard security requirements that were not designed to be specifically appropriate.

In the second worst scenario, they may expect the business to refrain from using the new technology altogether.

Anything, other than embracing and finding ways to secure these new technologies by design from the outset, will lead to security gaps for an organization.

These gaps can easily provide megabreach-sized opportunities.

One of the most frequent examples of how this occurs involves safe file transfers. To help protect an organization, the security function often designs rules and restrictions to help prevent massive and unsafe transfers of bulk information.

If part of an organization has a requirement, regular or one-off, to transfer a supernormal amount of information to an outside party, it should, in the first instance, contact the security function and ask for help to safely achieve the objective.

If the security department declines to help, or only offers a time frame that would result in substantial business costs or disruptions, it encourages the individuals involved to find a workaround.

Security workarounds are just as dangerous as they sound.

There is no shortage of file transfer technologies available via the Internet. Some of them are cheap, some are free, some are expensive, some have great security, some do not. Even if a technology is potentially secure, it usually requires some configuration to be performed by both the sender and receiver to ensure that the contents cannot be intercepted or copied.

What this demonstrates is that any security department that spends its time focusing on what it considers to be easily achievable and deflecting or putting aside internal requests for rapid and safe adoption of new technology can be sure it is creating the right conditions for a breach with potentially significant brand damage.

It only takes the exposure of a single document, such as one containing financial results not yet officially released to the market, to create this type of damage.

So think about it. Does your security department have processes in place to help rapidly assess and securely provide the technologies the organization requires?

Stacked Risk: The Danger of Silos

Megabreaches can only happen when three or more critical and major gaps in security can be leveraged to get to a major system.

Those three gaps are not usually found in the same major or critical system. They are usually at different layers and places across the security landscape. Just like finding a route through a maze, attackers look for a small combination of gaps to find their way in.

If individual risks or security deficits are only considered in isolation, the outcome is misleading. It may appear that the potential impact will be much less than the reality will reveal.

The usual symptom of this type of isolated approach is that the security of an organization is managed in silos, without overall management. The security department will lack the capability and will often lack the will to aggregate their risk and gap information.

If you have competing security teams, with each safeguarding and justifying their own budget and each managing their own risks in isolation, the organization will have an inaccurate perception of the true level of risk.

Only a fully accountable, single security function – with full visibility and control over the risk landscape – will have the ability to put in place adequate protection.

Take a look at where your security function is. Is there more than one security department? Are they under separate management reporting structures? Does the security function report to any person or committee other than the main board where the CEO sits?

If you can answer 'yes' to any of these questions, then your organization's security approach is fractured and disconnected in ways that cyber attackers can exploit.

Security only has the potential to work effectively when it is fully and transparently managed by cybersecurity people who comprise a clearly-defined chain of command, with a single point of accountability that reports directly to the main board. Only departments that use this method of security management are able to accurately pull together the risk picture and to correctly prioritize the actions required to build and sustain security.

Agile or Fragile?

Without a single, centrally accountable security function that reports directly to (or sits on) the main executive board, the likelihood is that you have all the ingredients for a megabreach already in place.

However, even if you do have such a function, it is still very easy for that function to manage security in a way that still allows large numbers of critical or major security gaps to persist.

Fragile, breakable security is easy to spot. This type of security does not adapt to changing times or conditions. It remains focused on what used to work and on what remains comfortable to sustain.

Just like a Captain of old going down with the ship, the management remains diligently at the helm steering the same course. After all, it has not failed to keep this Captain in his post thus far.

Most cyber attacks, especially those that result in megabreaches, have little to do with using cutting-edge techniques. Most attacks take advantage of vulnerabilities that have had fixes available for some time; it is simply that those fixes have never been applied to that particular system or environment.

According to a wide range of available statistics, the security expenditures of many organizations continue to be disproportionately allocated toward internal networks. Protecting the internal network layer does little to protect all of the devices and information that travel outside it and those internal network security measures can often not even differentiate between good and bad traffic inside. Spending disproportionately on internal network often means the security areas that need greater investment are left underfunded and open to intrusion.

Although the majority of security professionals do understand that every application and electronic information store needs security embedded by design and should be regularly assessed, re-tested and updated, only a minority of security departments apply this practice in the real world.

It is also widely known and accepted that new exploits, such as zero-day vulnerabilities, are being discovered on a daily basis. Although there are plenty of security technologies and processes that can be used to defend cyber systems against these threats, it is again only a minority of companies that look to have active defenses against them.

Just because an exploit is new does not mean it is impossible to counteract the risks it presents. Rapid patch management (applying fixes within hours of their availability) is one example of this kind of defense. However, as already mentioned, there are also new kinds of security technologies, including the latest anti-malware endpoint detection, that can identify and block over 99% of brand new threats before they can do anything.

Running outdated technology; having unpatched, unchecked hardware and software; maintaining fragmented management and security status reporting processes; and ignoring opportunities to identify and address root causes of security incidents are all symptoms that the security of an organization is fragile.

Disruptions for the staff and customers trying to use the systems are another symptom of fragile security, and one that is too often considered acceptable.

One reason many security functions consider the consequences of fragile security to be acceptable is that they do not understand that agile security is considerably cheaper than the outdated practices outlined above.

Getting to a robust security position requires a holistic and comprehensive approach. It requires a full set of processes that enable the business to swiftly identify and get security layered into their technologies – and re-checked on a regular basis.

It also has a fundamental requirement that the security function remembers to start at the information layer itself.

One security architect took me through his plan. He had adopted a great model from NIST (the US National Institute for Standards & Technology). That model looked to consider all the opportunities to detect, deny, disrupt and destroy threats.

His model was pretty good, as far as it went – but it had two major shortcomings. The first issue was that because his organization had no accurate and complete understanding of its applications of value, the architecture was designed around the gaps. It was notably focused on placing as many network and endpoint (laptop, desktop and mobile) defenses as possible. It then took a very light approach to the security requirements on the applications themselves.

As there was no central identity and access management capability, the architecture had to avoid including it.

However, that was not the biggest omission.

'What about security items for the information layer itself?' I asked.

Although the architecture had considered many security layers, it had not looked at the most vital component. It missed critical items like placing encryption and cryptographic key management into the design.

It was not that this security architect was not capable of creating an effective and comprehensive design. However, he had explicit instructions to work around the gaps.

As ever, my mind wandered back to those beautiful, carbon black security doors from chapter one – and the wide-open wooden fire exit door on the side.

It is easy to spend a lot of money on security – but only coordinating the approach across a full digital landscape will achieve effective security.

People Hate the Company

One of the most surprising patterns that emerges from reviewing security in so many different organizations is how the culture translates into the security position.

After dozens of reviews, I began to notice that organizations in which internal personnel did not get along and were openly disgruntled about the company would always end up with the most substantial set of security deficiencies.

Typically, employees in these companies felt threatened by and mistrusted each other. They would hide information from each other, and this, in turn, would allow any problems to remain hidden until, or unless, these problems resulted in fairly epic failures.

Conversely, in situations where the culture was open and supportive, the spirit of collaboration was infectious. People would work together to safeguard the company's wider interests.

While companies with great culture did not always have great security, they at least had the capacity for far more agility in understanding and addressing their issues.

Sometimes, though, a positive culture would go too far and result in extreme – and dangerous – levels of trust.

In fact, although discord among internal personnel always leads to a wealth of open security gaps, overly trusting environments that lack regular security checks and balances can lead to a similar position.

The difference between a company with a positive culture and one with a negative culture is that in workplaces in which people love the organization, they actively seek to protect it.

Thus, two organizations may have the same security gaps – but the one with internal personnel who seek to protect the company will have the support to manually address its problems.

Some of the most secure by design environments I have ever seen are due to the companies being hardened by continuous attacks. Hacktivists hate them, some of their customers don't like them, and worse still, their employees feel like disadvantaged commodities. But repeated attacks and compromises force them to be reasonably secure.

But even relatively secure organizations with unhappy employees may stir up security vulnerabilities when the organization is undergoing substantial changes that make employees feel even more undervalued. Staff in those types of environments will openly discuss the security problems, and this can make it relatively easy for hackers to access company information.

There is a culture curve that relates to security. Fostering a positive, supportive and sharing culture pays dividends – but it is not the only factor that is needed to protect an organization's cybersecurity. An ongoing, sustained level of independent, professional review is also required to ensure that security processes remain robust.

So if you want to know if your organization has a megabreach brewing – it is a relatively simple thing to identify:

- Are information assets all routinely recorded into a central inventory?
- Is there a really slick and simple single username and password in use across all the systems you access?
- Is the organization able to adopt new technology through processes that provide fast access to the security requirements and checks from the very beginning?
- Are technologies re-assessed for their security on a regular basis – and are any fixes put in place quickly?
- Is the CISO (or equivalent) reporting directly to the CEO or sitting on the main executive board alongside the CEO?
- Does the organization have a positive culture that encourages security problems to be reported – resulting in swift action to address the problems?
- Are patches to devices and operating systems deployed with lightning speed?

If you answered 'yes' to all of these questions – you are working for one of the few organizations that has little to no chance of suffering a megabreach.

10: Utopian Cybersecurity

'So if you don't fix the root causes, the symptoms will just re-occur.'

The tight-lipped look on the face of the security manager I was talking with told me in no uncertain terms that was not how they rolled.

They did their own thing, and months later, the root problems were persisting. As fast as the security team was mopping up issues, new ones were being spilled onto the floor.

Another meeting of the same people was called to examine how to fix the problems. This meeting reminded of my favorite support comeback line:

'Wait a second. So you're telling me you didn't do what I said and it still isn't working?'

There are many excellent security professionals out there. They are ready to do the right tasks. All you need is a correctly skilled and motivated Chief Information Security Officer at the helm, reporting directly to the main executive board. If you ensure you have a knowledgeable and accountable security leader at the helm, reporting directly to the main executive board, and regular, independent and unbiased audits, great security is a reachable and affordable goal.

Great security is possible. No organization has to live with the fear that they could be taken out by a megabreach at any time.

This is what effective security looks like:

The business departments and employees in an organization consider the company's security position to be both an advantage and an enabler of business success. When they want a new technology or need to manage a new set of information, there are simple-to-use processes that can immediately be accessed and put in motion.

They can answer some easy questions, record some basic information and all of the follow-up processes are pre-set to happen like clockwork.

If what they are doing is really new, they will be assigned a security expert to help them understand the new requirements. If these new requirements are likely to recur with subsequent new technologies, the security expert will build them into the existing easy to access and use processes.

Whenever a new vulnerability is identified, the technologies in which the potential exploits exist are fixed within 24 hours.

Using the security management reporting protocols, the executive can ask any question about security and receive a response in something close to real time. When all of the security information is stored into a single framework, it is easy to understand and access for status reports.

As a new employee, when I first start, I am not trained to be a layer of security. I am trained to be vigilant and to know how to report security issues and access processes anytime I need some new technology or need to collect and manage any new type of electronic information.

I arrive at my desk and boot up my laptop. I can surf anywhere I please, safe in the knowledge that the active layers of security will handle any threats that are thrown at them.

I have been trained not to do stupid things like disclosing personal or company information. I know that I should avoid clicking on anything in an unsolicited message – but even if I do, the chances it will contribute to an incident are negligible. After all, my laptop has the latest advanced anti-malware that even modified threats stand little chance of getting past.

Even if these threats bypass the anti-malware, my organization's security is robust by design. I cannot download or transfer bulk information without going through the right checks, balances and additional approvals.

All the sensitive information is encrypted anyway.

Whenever there is an incident, which are typically minor anyway, the security department is straight on the problem and view it as an opportunity to further augment their security processes and architecture to prevent the problem from recurring.

I can seamlessly use all of the applications I need to without re-entering any information. After all, my organization runs a single, super-intelligent identity and access management system that can recognize and block any errant behavior. This system would detect an attempted intrusion by comparing a hacker's location to my location, whether I had logged off my computer seconds, minutes, or hours ago. It would not give someone in an impossibly faraway location access.

This identity and access management system knows more than just my password. It can recognize me through a wide range of unique features from my face to my voice to the pass I carry and the equipment I use.

If you think that this description is about a dream world, it is worth stating that all of these technologies exist, and some organizations have already implemented this kind of approach. Unfortunately, in early 2017, this type of security is not yet the norm; it is the exception that has been installed for under one percent of organizations.

When I reflect on the purpose of this book – it is to make it clear that the idea that security is difficult to achieve has some truth to it. But the idea that great security is impossible is total hogwash.

Any organization experiencing a megabreach may be able to generate a long list of truisms to hide behind:

- You cannot fully protect everything all the time.
- There are always new threats.
- This attack was due to a zero-day exploit.

Yes – all of these are correct but none of them are an adequate excuse for a megabreach.

Great security is simply about having a comprehensive and orchestrated approach, with processes that start by capturing any information of value that needs to be protected.

Security is not achievable through a set of fixed technical controls. There is no set and static list of technologies and configuration options, but there are processes and objectives that can be used to implement and dynamically sustain the right protection.

Hackers and other attackers simply look for a target organization that has one or more of the long and growing list of possible vulnerabilities that can be exploited. When a security department constantly remains aware and stays on top of the necessary defenses, the gaps are not large enough to benefit an attacker.

When security is embedded by design, it is thousands of times cheaper to manage and hundreds of times more effective than trying to take an ad-hoc approach. Best of all, it can never result in a devastating megabreach.

The Cyber House Rules are a simple starting point to help organizations understand that many of the problems are rooted in the past.

The sheer pace of change means that security is not a paint that can be applied later on. It has to be locked into everything that is required of every critical technology that is used, even when that technology is not managed inside a corporate network.

Often, a security colleague at a conference will present me with what he or she considers to be an impossible problem. His or her perception that the problem is either difficult or impossible to solve results from past experience.

For example, when a new and critical Linux vulnerability was discovered, one security delegate said to me, 'There is no way any large organization could identify all of the servers where this new Linux vulnerability needs to be patched.'

That may have been true for this individuals' own organization, but the issue is not that this was unachievable. If their security function had an accurate information asset inventory, linked to the applications on which the information resided and to the hardware on which it ran, the identification of the servers requiring patching would be easily accessible in the form of a report that could be generated with a few clicks.

They could even have prioritized the remediation work based on the value of the services each of the servers was providing.

If you want to know the real reason that cybersecurity is so exposed, it has to do with the impact the rate of technological change has on how we need to work. That rate of change requires fundamental changes to how security is applied. We cannot take shortcuts and ignore any layer that needs security. We have to move from a network-centric approach to embedding security into every layer:

- On the electronic information.
- On the applications.
- On the devices.
- On the communication routes.
- On cloud services.
- On supplier systems.
- …

If you miss one layer, this opens vulnerability opportunities for cyber attackers to exploit. If you keep using a security technology or technique that is outdated, or fail to swiftly respond to a new type of attack, again, this opens the opportunities for attack.

A robust environment can survive with one or two open vulnerabilities for a short amount of time. It cannot avoid megabreaches if many substantial gaps are left open for long periods of time.

We were educated to operate security cost-efficiently by taking shortcuts. We never used to have to think about everywhere the electronic information of value might go. Although the many security frameworks such as those offered by ISACA COBIT, NIST, COSO and others always required us to think this way – in the real world, real security was often run using a nickel and dime approach that entailed implementing safety nets like network security.

At that time, this approach provided adequate protection.

Now it does not.

Utopian cybersecurity is achieved by taking adequate care to cover the full digital ecosystem. It requires consideration of security wherever the information of value flows. It also means that there are times when not allowing information to flow somewhere is the right course of action.

The biggest failure of some of the emergent security techniques is that they promote the idea that detection and recovery is a primary approach. Detection and recovery are essential capabilities – but they are also a last resort.

The more these last resort processes are triggered – the bigger the gaps in the primary defenses are.

If you *need* a massive staff to manage the repeated recovery of disrupted and contaminated devices, this is not a sign that you have excellent security; it is in fact a sign that your primary defenses are terrible.

Again, I have seen this in real-world examples. Consider two companies with similar multi-billion dollar turnovers. One runs security by design with a full range of security processes and an architecture that requires a single identity and access verification for all key systems. The other uses a fragmented approach, mopping up ad-hoc issues very slowly and expensively.

The budget of the security by design organization is half the one of their counterpart. This company has a small in-house security team, with a flexible outsource arrangement to run a recovery if needed.

Their counterpart has tens of staff fire-fighting the intrusions and desperately recruiting more team members as fast as they can.

The company running security by design is using a platform I designed. Its security department can identify in real-time the footprint from any zero-day exploit in a few clicks.

The other company runs without anything like this capability. Identifying the footprint of any zero-day vulnerability is a major project that takes at least many months, and even then it misses items.

The company running security by design can meet data privacy regulations with no changes. It can identify exactly where personal information is held. Security personnel know that this information is automatically checked and reassessed every year – and that all of the information is required to be encrypted.

The company running ad-hoc processes leaves issues like data privacy regulations to its business units and tells its executive that the approach being used is standard for the industry. It doesn't get independently audited – and the executive trusts that what the security people are saying is correct.

Into the Future

Most of us – both individuals and organizations – have pitiful security in place. Because of this, we can expect cybercrime to continue to grow for awhile – but soon the cybercrime revolution will be quelled.

The huge growth in cybercrime has relied on cryptocurrency for funding and on security with plenty of gaps in place to perpetuate the opportunities for criminals to exploit others.

The tables are about to turn.

Whether or not cryptocurrency can be defeated is uncertain. I hope this unaccountable and unregulated method of finance is consigned to history – but it may well survive and become the global currency of the future.

However, security technology is fortunately evolving very quickly.

In 2017, although robust security depends on security by design, an increasing number of technologies offer new safety nets. As those new technologies are adopted, even if there are substantial gaps, there should be enough preventive technologies deployed to stop the problems.

Even the latest endpoint security now has the capability to stop almost all threats from malicious software from being effective.

The computing we are all used to is also about to end. People will look back at all the physical screens and passwords in the same way that we look back on typewriters and filing cabinets.

The hyper-connected world we now live in is about to get even more hyper-connected. The speed and diversity of connection options will increase. Technologies will know exactly who each user is. Even passers-by will know exactly who everyone who walks near them is.

Technology is moving at such a fast pace that even the security of this technology will soon be managed mostly by other computers.

Until then, we all need to hold companies that run their cybersecurity badly to account. Security is only run badly when an organization's decision-makers consider badly-run security to be acceptable.

Megabreaches do not need to happen. This book has aimed to explain both the reasons that they exist and how they can be swiftly defeated.

There are plenty of actions we can all take to make this a reality.

Whether as an employee or a customer, for your own best interests, abandon organizations that pay ransomware or that suffer repeated breaches.

If you are a manager or a senior executive, do what you can to change up your organization's mindset so the security function and the executive board are motivated to implement the right practices and to ensure that security is put in place where it needs to be.

Every megabreach is preventable.

Cyber criminals and other hackers who succeed are not cleverly navigating complex walls of digital security; they are walking through gaps they could literally drive a truck through.

Security is not a paint that can be applied later on. Effective security requires the right measures to be included by design from the outset.

Boardroom politics, the realities of risk management and human psychology are all playing their part to encourage organizations to leave their security out-dated and broken.

Information is the new security perimeter.

Great security is more than possible. Megabreaches are a symptom of poor security practices and not the acceptable result of impossible risk management that many security functions pretend they are.

The risks are manageable with the right approaches.

Security professionals will give you what you need, if you provide them with the motivation, training, oversight and resources they need. All that is needed is to consistently apply security by design to all of the technology and process layers.

Cybersecurity to English

This section is an abridged version of the separate publication 'The **Cybersecurity to English Dictionary'**. It contains only key terms used in this book.

The full version of this dictionary is available as a separate publication.

anti-malware – *is a computer program designed to look for specific files and behaviors* (**signatures**) *that indicate the presence or the attempted installation of malicious software. If or when detected, the program seeks to isolate the attack (quarantine or block the* **malware**), *remove it, if it can, and also alert appropriate people to the attempt or to the presence of the malware.*

anti-virus – *predecessor of* **anti-malware** *software that was used before the nature and types of malicious software had diversified. This is a computer program designed to look for the presence or installation of specific files. If or when detected, the program seeks to isolate the attack (quarantine or block the* **virus**), *remove it, if it can, and also alert appropriate people to the attempt. A virus is only one form of malware, so the term anti-malware is considered to be more inclusive of other forms of malicious software. However, as people are more familiar with the term 'anti-virus,' this can sometimes be used to describe some types of anti-malware. See also* **anti-malware** *and* **virus.**

advanced persistent threats (APTs) – *a term used to describe the tenacious and highly evolved set of tactics used by hackers to infiltrate* **networks** *through* **digital devices** *and to then leave malicious software in place for as long as possible. The* **cyber attack lifecycle** *usually involves the attacker performing research & reconnaissance, preparing the most effective attack tools, getting an initial foothold into the network or target* **digital landscape**, *spreading the infection and then adjusting the range of the attack tools in place and exploiting the position to maximum advantage. The purpose can be to steal, corrupt, extort and/ or disrupt an organization for financial gain, brand damage or political purposes. This form of sophisticated attack becomes harder and more costly to resolve, the further into the lifecycle the attackers are and the longer the attack tools have already remained in place. A goal with this threat type is for the intruder to remain (persist) undetected for as long as possible in order to maximize the opportunities presented by the intrusion – for example, the opportunity to steal data over a long period of time. See also* **kill-chain.**

artificial intelligence – *the development of knowledge and skills in computer programs* (**applications**) *to the extent that they are able to perform perception, recognition, translation and / or decision-making activities without prior direct experience with an event.*

attack surface – *the sum of the potential exposure areas that could be used to gain unauthorized entry to, or extraction of, information.*

backup – *(i) the process of archiving a copy of something so that it can be restored following a disruption. (ii) having a redundant (secondary) capability to continue a process, service or application if the primary capability is disrupted.*

Bitcoin – *a decentralized, virtual digital currency* (**cryptocurrency**) *and payment system, based on a distributed, public ledger. The currency provides a high degree of transactional anonymity as balances and ledger entries* are associated with private cryptographic keys and not with the individual or company that uses it (lose your key, lose your money). This has made it, along with other digital currencies, a payment method of choice for criminals, who also use it to make and receive cyber blackmail payments. The invention of Bitcoin is also associated with the invention of a sophisticated encryption-based authenticity technique known as **blockchain**. *See also* **blockchain**.

black hat – a person who engages in attempts to gain unauthorized access to one or more digital devices with nefarious (criminal or unethical) objectives. A **hacker** with unethical goals, or no perceived ethical goals.

blockchain – a method developed as part of the **cryptocurrency** system known as **Bitcoin** to authenticate valid transactions. A distributed, public ledger of transactions is created, with each new entry leveraging an encrypted hash value from the last entry in the ledger. This means that the ledger is stronger than previously designed authenticity techniques. Theoretical falsification of an entry would require the encryption to not only be broken or changed, but also the full sequence of entries in all public copies of the ledger to be adjusted. This technique (and a private variation) is now expected to be widely adopted as a standard method for authenticity across digital platforms where authenticity is required.

botnet – shortened version of *robotic network*. A connected set of programs designed to operate together over a network (including the Internet) to achieve specific purposes. The purpose can be good or bad. Some programs of this type are used to help support Internet connections, but malicious uses include taking over control of some or all of a computer's functions to support large-scale service attacks (see **denial of service**). Botnets are sometimes referred to as *zombie armies*.

Business Continuity Plan – (abbreviation BCP). An operational document that describes how an organization can restore their critical products or services to their customers should a substantial event that causes disruptions to normal operations occur.

BYOC – acronym for **B**ring **Y**our **O**wn **C**loud. A term used to describe the **cybersecurity** status in which employees or contractors are making direct decisions to use externally hosted services to manage, at least part of, their organization's work. If this is taking place without the inclusion of a process to assess any risks and to control the security features, it can lead to significant risks both to the direct information involved and by potentially opening up other security gaps in the **digital landscape**.

Chief Information Security Officer (CISO) – a single point of accountability in any organization for ensuring that an appropriate and effective framework for managing dangers and threats is operating and effective.

CISO – see **Chief Information Security Officer**.

clopen – a network or system that is intended to be run as closed and secure but due to size, scale, threats or security deficiencies is constantly identifying and seeking to eliminate new intrusions. A portmanteau of the words **clo**sed and **open**.

containerization – (i) the partitioning of software functions within a single device sufficient to isolate it from potential harm or other unwanted interaction from other software on the same device. (ii) the complete isolation of one technology from another.

control – (in the context of security and compliance) a method of regulating something, often a process, technology or behavior, to achieve a desired outcome, usually resulting in the reduction of risk. Depending on how it is designed and used, any single control may be referred to as preventive, detective or corrective.

cryptocurrency – *any digital currency that makes use of* **encryption** *to generate and secure confidence in the units that are traded. These forms of payment are usually decentralized, unregulated and their ownership is difficult to trace, making them the main form of payment for cyber crime and ransomware. See also* **Bitcoin** *and* **blockchain**.

cyber attack – *to take aggressive or hostile action by leveraging or targeting* **digital devices***. The intended damage is not limited to the digital (electronic) environment.*

cyber attack lifecycle – *a conceptual model of the sequential steps that are involved in a successful unauthorized intrusion or disruption into a* **digital landscape** *or* **digital device***. There are a number of models currently available; an example of the most common steps found across the models is illustrated in the definition of* **advanced persistent threat***. See also* **kill chain***.*

cybercrime – *the act of violating the laws of one or more countries through the illicit use or access to one or more digital technologies.*

cyber criminal – *any person who attempts to gain unauthorized access to one or more* **digital devices***.*

cyber physical systems – *combinations of devices that can work together through self-learning, computer-based algorithms to integrate their functions, authorized users and resources. They can use their transdisciplinary capabilities to address problems in real time. As an example – such a system may know how to set up new network connections or how to shut off anything determined to be rogue. A component of* **Industry 4.0***.*

cybersecurity – *the protection of* **digital devices** *and their communication channels to keep them stable, dependable and reasonably safe from danger or threat. Usually the required protection level must be sufficient to prevent or address unauthorized access or intervention before it can lead to substantial personal, professional, organizational, financial and/ or political harm.*

data governance – *the management of electronic information through the use of* **policies** *and* **procedures** *designed to ensure that transactions and storage are handled with appropriate care.*

data loss prevention (DLP) – *this term can describe both (i) technologies and (ii) the strategies used to help stop information from being taken out of an organization without the appropriate authorization. Software technologies can use heuristics (patterns that fit within certain rules), to recognize, raise alerts and/ or block data extraction activities on digital devices; for example, to prohibit specific types of file attachments from being sent out via Internet mail services. They can also prevent or monitor many other attempts at removing or copying data. There are workarounds that can be used by skilled hackers that can evade detection by these solutions, including encryption and fragmentation. Although these solutions are becoming an essential line of defense, the most secure environments aim to prevent any significant set of data being available for export in the first place. For this reason, data loss prevention is often thought of as the last line of defense (a final safety net if all other security controls have not been successful). Information loss prevention (ILP) is an alternative version of the same term.*

DDoS – *acronym for* **Distributed Denial of Service***. See* **Denial of Service** *for definition.*

Denial of Service (DoS) – *an attack designed to stop or disrupt people from using certain organizations' systems. Usually a particular section of an enterprise is targeted, for example, a specific network, system, digital device type or function. Usually these attacks originate from, and are targeted at, devices accessible through the*

Internet. *If the attack is from multiple source locations, it is referred to as a distributed denial of service or* **DDoS** *attack.*

digital device *– any electronic appliance that can create, modify, archive, retrieve or transmit information in an electronic format. Desktop computers, laptops, tablets, smartphones and Internet-connected home devices are all examples of* **digital devices.**

digital landscape *– the collection of* **digital devices** *and electronic information that is visible or accessible from a particular location.*

dwell-time *– in the context of* **cybersecurity** *– how long an intrusion or threat has been allowed to remain in place before being discovered and eliminated.*

employee led cloud adoption *– a form of* **shadow IT** *where people working for an organization take it upon themselves to start using Internet-based services without going through official routes for assessing and configuring the usage to a secure standard. See also* **BYOC.**

encryption *– the act of encoding messages so that if intercepted by an unauthorized party, they cannot be read unless the encoding mechanism can be deciphered.*

exploit *– to take advantage of a security* **vulnerability***. Well-known exploits are often given names. Falling victim to a known exploit with a name can be a sign of deficient security, such as poor* **patch management***.*

firewall *– is hardware (physical device) or software (computer program) used to monitor and protect inbound and outbound data (electronic information). It achieves this by applying a set of rules. These physical devices or computer programs are usually deployed, at a minimum, at the perimeter of each network access point. Software firewalls can also be deployed on devices to add further security. The rules applied within a firewall are known as the firewall policy.*

governance *– the methods used by any executive to keep their organization on track with the management goals and within acceptable performance standards. This is usually achieved by establishing* **policies***,* **procedures** *and* **controls** *that match the enterprise's vision, strategy and risk appetite.*

grey hat *– a hacker who does not have the overt, unethical intentions of a* **black hat** *but still makes use of techniques and tactics that are illegal. This type of hacker intends to make use of some unethical practices to help deliver ethical goals. See also* **white hat***.*

hacker *– a person who engages in attempts to gain unauthorized access to one or more digital devices.*

hacktivism *– an amalgamation of hacker and activism. Describes the act of seeking unauthorized access into any digital device or digital landscape to promote a social or political agenda. Usually the unauthorized access is used to cause destruction, disruption and/or publicity. Individuals participating in these acts are called* **hacktivists.**

hacktivist *– an amalgamation of the words hacker and activist. Describes any individual who participates in* **hacktivism.**

hashing *– using a mathematical function to convert any block or group of data into a fixed length value (usually shorter than the original data) that represents the original data. This fixed length value can be used for fast indexing of large files by computer programs without the need to manage the larger data block. It is also used* *extensively in the field of security; for example, digital forensics professionals can use this technique to verify that the data content of a copy of any examined data is identical to the original source.*

IDAM *– acronym for **Id**entify and **A**ccess **M**anagement - the collection of processes and technologies used to manage, confirm, monitor and control legitimate access to systems by authorized accounts. This includes measures to ensure each access request is from a verified, expected and legitimate person or entity.*

indicators of compromise (IOC) *– is a term originally used in computer forensics to describe any observable behaviors and patterns (such as particular blocks of data, registry changes, IP address references) that strongly suggest a computer intrusion has occurred or is taking place. The collation of these patterns and behaviors is now actively used in advanced threat defense to help security professionals more rapidly identify potential security issues from across a monitored digital landscape.*

Industry 4.0 *– the use of advanced technologies, such as cloud computing and distributed I**nternet of Things** devices, to deliver adaptable manufacturing and services at scale. The modular, intelligent and flexible nature of the approach permits continuous dynamic adjustment and improvement of the items contributing to the end product or service.*

Internet of Things (IoT) *– the incorporation of electronics into everyday items, sufficient to allow them to network (communicate) with other network-capable devices. For example, to include electronics in a home thermostat so that it can be operated and share information over a network connection to a smartphone or other network-capable device.*

Intrusion Prevention Systems (IPS) *– computer programs that monitor and inspect electronic communications that pass through them, with the purpose and ability (i) to detect, block and log (record key information) about any known malicious or otherwise unwanted streams of information and (ii) to log and raise alerts about any other traffic that is suspected (but not confirmed) to be of a similar nature. These programs are usually placed in the communication path to allow the prevention (dropping or blocking of packets) to occur; for example, within advanced firewalls. They can also clean some electronic data to remove any unwanted or undesirable packet components.*

kill chain *– a conceptual cyber defense model that uses the structure of attack as a model to build a cyber defense strategy. The stages in an **advanced persistent threat** are typically used as a framework. The model works on the assumption that the earlier in the lifecycle (kill chain) a threat is detected and defeated, the easier and lower the cost incurred to manage it.*

machine learning *– the ability for a software program to review sets of information and extrapolate new theories or patterns that were not pre-programmed. This is essentially an advanced form of pattern recognition fused with an early type of **artificial intelligence**. Programs with this capability can review and understand much larger sets of electronic information than humans can, and also have the ability to identify new trends and patterns and to then propose new findings or opportunities. This is proving to be sometimes beneficial, but has also raised controversies. One of the early issues that has emerged is that machine learning can reflect the bias or quality of the data and lacks the ethics of a human reviewer. For example, an undisclosed fraud review machine learning program proposed profiling each claimant's country of origin as an indicator of the likelihood of fraud. As with regular forms of statistical analysis, care has to be taken with how the program interprets correlations; in this case, if a key data point is missing, the wrong conclusion will be drawn. As a simple example - do I live in a certain country because I am overweight, am I overweight because I live in a certain country, or what other undisclosed factors may be involved?*

---

malware – *shortened version of* **malicious software**. *A disruptive, subversive or hostile program placed onto a* **digital device**. *These types of programs are usually disguised or embedded in a file that looks initially harmless, but is actually designed to compromise a device or network of devices. There are many types of malware – adware,* **botnets**, **computer viruses**, *ransomware,* **scareware**, **spyware**, *trojans and worms are all examples of malware. Cyber criminals often use malware to mount cybersecurity attacks.*

megabreach – *the term used to describe a* **cyber attack** *that involves such a high level of catastrophic theft and/or such extensive intrusion that it leads to worldwide media exposure. As the frequency and scale of breaches has increased, the threshold for calling an event newsworthy has also increased.*

Mobile Device Management (MDM) – *a technology used for the security administration of mobile devices such as tablets and smartphones. Able (for example) to remotely wipe information from a mobile device and to control which applications and functions are permitted to be installed or run.*

networks – *the name for a group of devices, wiring and applications used to connect, carry, broadcast, monitor or safeguard data. Networks can be physical (and use material assets such as wiring) or virtual (and use applications to create associations and connections between devices or applications.) Usually, the devices on a network will have some form of trusted permissions that allow them to pass and share packets of electronic information. This can be used as a route for spreading malicious software.*

patch management – *a controlled process used to deploy critical, interim updates to software on digital devices. The release of a software 'patch' usually occurs in response to a critical flaw or gap that has been identified. A failure to apply new interim software updates promptly can leave security* **vulnerabilities** *in place. As a consequence, promptly applying these updates (**patch management**) is considered a critical component of maintaining effective cybersecurity.*

phishing – *sending an electronic communication (for example email or instant messaging) that pretends to come from a legitimate source, in an attempt to get sensitive information (for example a password or credit card number) from the recipient or to install* **malware** *on the recipient's device. Phishing methods have evolved so the message can simply contain a link to an Internet location where malware is situated or can include an attachment (such as a PDF or Word document) that installs malware when opened. The malware can then be used to run any number of unauthorized functions, including stealing information from the device, replicating other malware to other accessible locations, sharing the user's screen and logging the user's keystrokes. Less complex forms of phishing may encourage the recipient to visit a fake but convincing version of a website and to disclose a password or other details.*

policy – *(i) a high-level statement of intent, often a short document, providing guidance on the principles an organization follows. For example, a basic security policy document could describe an enterprise's intention to ensure that all locations (physical and electronic) which contain information for which the company is accountable must remain secure from any unauthorized access. A policy does not usually describe the explicit mechanisms or specific instructions that would be used to achieve or enforce the intentions it expresses; this would be described in a* **procedure**. *(ii) Alternatively, it can also be used to refer to the settings (including security settings) inside a software program or operating system.*

port – *a physical or virtual connection point that helps organize the diverse range of communications and services that can take place between electronic devices and computer programs. Assigning a specific value (a port number) when sending information lets the recipient know what type of information it is and how to process it. This information can also be used by security devices such as* **firewalls** *to allow or deny certain communication types.*

procedure – *provides guidance or specific instruction on the process (method) that should be used to achieve an objective. Traditionally provided as a document available to appropriate personnel, but increasingly replaced by enforcing steps in computer systems. In a traditional quality model, procedures may reside under a* **policy** *as explicit instructions for meeting a particular policy objective. See also* **policy** *definition (i).*

rainbow tables – *a set of pre-computed encryption values that can be used to reverse engineer items such as hash values back to their unencrypted value. These can be used to help crack (reveal) an encrypted value. As an example, most short hash values that use standard hash techniques can be entered into Google to reveal their unencrypted value.*

router – *a device used to define the path for data packets (electronic information) to follow when they flow between networks.*

security architecture – *a model designed to specify the features and controls across a* **digital landscape** *that help a security system prevent, detect and control any attempts at disruption or unauthorized access.*

shadow IT – *technology that is adopted by an organization without going through official assessment and approval to ensure the correct security is in place. See also* **employee led cloud adoption** *and* **BYOC**.

signatures – *(in the context of cybersecurity) are the unique attributes, for example, file size, file extension, data usage patterns and method of operation, that identify a specific computer program. Traditional* **antimalware** *and other security technologies can make use of this information to identify and manage some forms of rogue software or communications.*

single point (of) failure – *a vulnerability that is so significant that it can be used to create a devastating disruption to an entire organization.*

smishing – *a phishing attack that uses the simple message service (SMS) to send a malicious link or file to a phone as a text message. If the malicious link or attachment is opened, the device may be compromised. This form of attack can also use the MMS (multi media service).*

social engineering – *The act of constructing relationships, friendships or other human interactions for the purpose of getting the victim to perform an action or to reveal information. The hidden purpose behind social engineering is that the criminal who engages in such acts uses the victim's action or the information revealed to achieve a nefarious objective, such as acquiring intelligence about the security, location or vulnerability of assets, or even gaining the person's trust so he or she will open an Internet link or document that will result in a* **malware** *foothold being created.*

spyware – *a form of malware that covertly gathers and transmits information from the device on which it is installed.*

stacked risk – *the phenomenon of allowing seemingly separate potential issues with potential impact (risks) affecting the same* **digital landscape** *to accumulate. Without adequate identification and resolution, individual risks can form a toxic accumulation of issues that can be leveraged together to create a risk that is substantially greater than the individual components suggest.* **Megabreaches** *are usually the result of stacked risks in combination with a motivated attacker.*

threat actors – *an umbrella term to describe the collection of people and organizations that work to create* **cyber attacks**. *Examples of threat actors can include* **cyber criminals**, **hacktivists** *and nation states.*

---

threatscape *– a term that amalgamates **threat** and land**scape**. An umbrella term that describes the overall, expected methods (vectors) and types of cyber attackers through or by which an organization or individual might expect to be attacked.*

TOR *– is a free software application designed to protect the anonymity of the people who use it. The name is an acronym for 'The Onion Router,' the project from which the application has continued to evolve and a reference to how the software operates. Communications use multiple layers of encryption that enable them to travel through multiple locations without ever revealing both the origination and destination points in any single step. At each step during the relay of the communication, only a single layer of the transmission route is revealed, with all the remaining layers remaining encrypted. The final **IP address** destination is only revealed by the very last layer. The IP address at which the communication originated is not revealed during any part of the communication relay, other than during the very first part. This mechanism is used to facilitate anonymous access to resources like the darknet.*

URL *– acronym for **u**niform **r**esource **l**ocator. This is essentially the address (or path) where a particular destination can be found. For example, the main address for the Google website is the URL http://www.google.com*

virtual private network (VPN) *– a method of providing a secure connection between two or more points over a public (or unsecure) infrastructure; for example, by setting up a secure link between a remote company laptop in a hotel and the main company network.*

virus *– a form of **malware** that spreads by infecting (attaching itself to) other files and that usually seeks opportunities to continue this pattern. Viruses are now less common than other forms of malware. Viruses were the main type of malware during the earliest years of computing. For this reason, people often refer to something as a virus when it is technically another form of malware.*

vishing *– abbreviation for **v**oice ph**ishing**. The use of a phone call or similar communication method (such as instant messaging) in which the caller attempts to deceive the recipient so he or she will perform an action (such as visiting a URL), or revealing information that can then be used to obtain unauthorized access to systems or accounts. Usually the ultimate purpose is to steal (or hold ransom) something of value. These types of calls are becoming extremely regular, as the criminal gangs involved may have stolen part of the recipient's data already (name, phone number, …) and may use this information to help persuade the person receiving the call that it is authentic. As a rule, if you did not initiate a call or message, you should never comply with any demand, especially one that instructs you to visit any webpage or link.*

VPN tunnel *– the secure communication route between two **VPN** connection points. See also **virtual private network**.*

vulnerability *– (in the context of cybersecurity) a weakness, usually in design, implementation or operation of software (including operating systems), that could be compromised and result in damage or harm.*

white-hat *– a security specialist who breaks into systems or networks by invitation (and with the permission) of the owner, with the intent to help identify and address security gaps.*

zero-day attack *– refers to the very first time a new type of exploit or new piece of malware is discovered. At that point in time, none of the anti-virus, anti-malware or other defenses may be set up to counteract the new form of exploit.*